'Miranda France's *Bad Times in Buenos Aires* [is] a complete surprise, and a wonderful one at that. Wonderful because her writing catches colour, rhythm, smog, smell and sadness in a way that few travel writers achieve today. And a complete surprise because Argentina is obviously about as different from Britain as it is possible for two countries to be ... France could not have found a country that was better suited to her gifts for visual observation and the nuance of language and its sub-texts' *Literary Review*

'*Bad Times in Buenos Aires* is an anguished love affair with a city put to mesmerising and compulsive prose by an obviously talented writer' *Glasgow Herald*

'Engagingly candid ... this is a penetrating portrait of Buenos Aires, full of devastating insights into the mood of a disturbed nation' *Catholic Herald*

'It is notoriously difficult to write a successful travel book if you have a bad time, but she pulls it off because she is such a good writer ... I loved this book. It shines a beam of light on to Buenos Aires, and illuminates a shadowy corner of the Argentinian psyche to boot' *Daily Telegraph*

'She writes so smoothly and effortlessly, painting with a few strokes of her pen an image so vivid that you find yourself transported to Buenos Aires. Hilarious and tragic ... Sensitive, colourful, imaginative and informed, the book has depth and poetry. Miranda France tells a compelling story and, by the end of it, I felt I had grasped the essence of the paradox that is Argentina' *Wanderlust*

Miranda France was born in 1966 and brought up in East Anglia and Sussex. She read Spanish and Latin American Studies at Edinburgh University. Invited to help organise a revolution in Peru by some communists she met in Madrid, she returned instead to university where she took a First in 1989. She lived in Brazil and Edinburgh, and then Buenos Aires between 1993 and 1995. In 1996 she won the Shiva Naipaul Memorial Prize for a piece about her time in Buenos Aires. She is married and lives in London where she works as a journalist. This is her first book.

Bad Times in Buenos Aires

MIRANDA FRANCE

PHOENIX

A Phoenix Paperback
First published in Great Britain
by Weidenfeld & Nicolson in 1998
This paperback edition published in 1999 by Phoenix,
a division of Orion Books Ltd,
Orion House, 5 Upper St Martin's Lane,
London WC2H 9EA

A CIP catalogue record for this book
is available from the British Library.

ISBN: 0 75380 551 0

Printed and bound in Great Britain by
The Guernsey Press Co. Ltd,
Guernsey, Channel Islands

The failure of Argentina, so rich, so under-populated, twenty-three million people in a million square miles, is one of the mysteries of our time.

V. S. NAIPAUL

I come from a sad country.

JORGE LUIS BORGES

To Carl Honoré

CONTENTS

1 Heat and Lust   1

2 Crossed Wires   18

3 A Nation on the Couch   37

4 The Wall of Silence   58

5 A Fear of Falling Buttocks   80

6 Evita Aflame   103

7 *Las Malvinas Son Argentinas*   128

8 Cake-fighting in Patagonia,
   and Other Travels   154

9 Call This a Democracy?   177

10 Going Home   196

Further Reading   208

ix

ACKNOWLEDGEMENTS

Many people in Argentina have helped with this book. I would particularly like to thank Raquel López Llames, a dear friend. My thanks also go to Pablo and Santiago Méndez Huergo, Hugo Palavecino, Guillermo Zerda, Martín Raffa, Manuel Santín, Uki Goñi and Sylvina Walger. In Britain, I thank my editor Benjamin Buchan for his generous help, Peter James for his astute suggestions, and my friends and family for their encouragement.

I am grateful to Penguin Books for permission to reproduce on page 35 part of the poem 'Daybreak' from Jorge Luis Borges, *Selected Poems 1923–1967*. The translation is by Norman Thomas di Giovanni. Some of the episodes in this book first appeared in the *Spectator*.

CHAPTER ONE

Heat and Lust

I ARRIVED IN A city that seemed fascinated by the possibility of its own collapse. 'We are in crisis!' declared the headline on one of the first newspapers I picked up – and it was true that an unspecified threat of chaos pervaded the city centre. The grand European architecture that had given Buenos Aires its cherished nickname, 'the Paris of the south', was in places relaxing into a dilapidation from which it might never be roused. Some of its many splendid domes had crumbled into the shoulders of buildings that refused to support them any longer. On the Avenida de Mayo, a once lofty spire had toppled to one side, so that now it pointed an accusing finger at the government buildings on the other side of the Plaza del Congreso.

Following the line of the fallen spire, that first afternoon in Buenos Aires, I found that the monument directly in front of the Congress had more particular allegations to make. It stood in the middle of the plaza, a large, strangely menacing edifice of stone and bronze. At the front of it, accompanied by a grotesque band of lizards, vultures and rearing horses, a muscular god stepped out of a shell into what should have been a splendid spray of water, except that the fountains to provide such a scene were defunct. It was a shame because, without the drama of water, the horses reared pointlessly, the thighs of the god rippled to no good purpose and the whole mythic accompaniment seemed thwarted. Rising behind this redundant scene was a column to commemorate Argentina's Independence. At its base sat a pair of bare-breasted muses, one displaying her broken chains with an expression of astonishment, while her companion held a horn of plenty, describing the fertility of the new republic.

The monument might once have looked grand, perhaps it had even persuaded patriotic hearts to leap, but now it was covered with graffiti designed to abash those politicians who dared look down from their windows in Congress. 'Traitors!', 'Assassins!' proclaimed the unsteady black ink, and 'Support the Pensioners!', 'Justice for the Disappeared!' One that made me stop cold in the outrageous heat was 'English out of the Malvinas!'

High above this summary of Argentine woes rose the third bronze muse, gazing thoughtfully from her column-top towards the sea, perhaps towards the Italian studio where she had been conceived. In one hand she held an olive branch that seemed to wilt in the heat. She had been made never to cast a backward glance, which was just as well, because she was most intimately defiled. Printed on her sloping buttocks were two words I was to see endlessly echoed on the walls of Buenos Aires, scrawled on monuments and in public lavatories, reproduced on leaflets and posters, until they came to embody a subtle tyranny. The words were 'Evita lives'.

It was just after lunch. In a grand old café near the Congress, clusters of elegant elderly women were drinking coffee out of tiny cups. The ladies were well powdered and lacquered and each had made of her hair a teased and sugary confection that looked like golden candyfloss. Through the stained-glass windows I could see that waiters in white jackets were serving the ladies patisserie with silver tongs. On the other side of the plaza, at tables shaded by trees, young people were drinking Coca-Cola. The fashion that summer was for youths of both sexes to wear their hair very long and neat, a smarter gender confusion than might be seen on the streets of London or New York. Young *porteños* – as the city's inhabitants were called – made no overt sign of rebellion; they were not multifariously tattooed or pierced. In fact they looked as sleek and glossy as otters, and they were well dressed and even adorned with gold. Some of them carried mobile telephones. I could not imagine that such well-washed heads were vexed by the Malvinas, the disappeared, by whether Evita lived or not.

And yet the monument in front of the Congress was not alone in its grievances: as I walked around Buenos Aires in the following days, I noticed that many statues bore the same scribbled complaints – they were an embittered lot, these sculpted heroes and heroines of Argentina's past. Three words appeared with particular regularity: *Asesinos. Corruptos. Traidores.* Who were these villains? What had they done?

In Buenos Aires, each morning's newspapers proclaimed a new catastrophe. Apparently the city's air pollution was dangerously in excess of what was permitted by the World Health Organization. If you were reckless enough to leave your baby unattended on the pavement, it would asphyxiate within fifteen minutes. Noise levels were twice what they should be. Every hour a driver died on the roads and every two hours someone was catapulted to his death by a broken lift. 'Not only does nothing work properly, but people can't breathe, they can't move and they can't hear,' said the head of the Argentine Ecological Movement on television. 'Something has to be done or we're going to explode!'

There were two novel ways to die that summer: one was to succumb to 'urban stress', a newly diagnosed killer which was causing sales of tranquillizers to soar. The other – less common, but more dramatic – was to fall into one of the deep holes that had opened up in pavements all over the city. These multiplying death-traps were the work of an army of low-paid immigrants engaged on a mission to tear out and replace the capital's guts from under its main roads. Stripped to the waist, they worked in pits alongside the pavements, chattering in a Paraguayan dialect that sounded like birdsong. In between drilling and digging, they were ideally placed to look up the passing women's skirts and to make suggestions, frustratingly unintelligible, about what they saw. At midday the men climbed out of their pits and slung huge cuts of meat on to a metal grid arranged over burning coals on the road. They ate the grilled meat with their hands, sitting on the kerb amid parked cars and traffic fumes, still laughing and chattering as they chewed.

People said the city was sinking. Of the 300 brands of condom in circulation, only eight were safe. The traffic was out of control: traffic lights failed. A newspaper poll revealed that 'most Argentines believe a car accident is an act of God, and cannot be avoided'. More than 2,000 bus drivers were found to be clinically depressed. Then there were the rats, whose number had soared from three million to twenty-four million in just a few years. In the capital alone, they were said to be eating four tons of food a day. 'For every one of us,' boasted a headline, 'there are eight rats.'

This collage of impressions, of proliferating rats, asphyxiating babies and life brutally snuffed out in lifts, coloured the atmosphere of my first few days in Buenos Aires. It was March when I arrived, and fiercely hot, but the humidity was much more devastating than the heat. At its worst, say at 98 per cent humidity, there was a terrible tension in the atmosphere. The air became thick and bulky, and one moved through it with difficulty, cutting a swathe through the congested city streets. I could easily imagine asphyxiating in such heat. It was uncomfortable to be outside, but then it was also uncomfortable to be indoors, to lie down, to eat or to drink. It was uncomfortable to be alive.

At bus stops and on television, the talk was of a summer that refused to make way for autumn; if anything the heat seemed to be intensifying and everyone agreed that the mini-skirts were getting shorter. The more scandalous versions, barely covering the groin, were a source of national marvel. A voyeuristic exercise dressed up as television debate promised to look *closely* at the question of rising hem-lines. Meanwhile, women tottered their assets around the streets on dangerously high heels while the watching men huffed and sighed like steam engines. Deep in their pits, the Paraguayan road diggers looked up the passing skirts and sweated. The streets seemed to hum with a male murmuring, a low chorus of *Dios Míos* and *Ay Madres*.

The heat addled and inebriated. One evening two buses, filled to capacity with commuters, collided below our window and I watched as the drivers dutifully descended into the street to swing punches at one another. Hoicking up trousers and rolling up sleeves, the men staked out an arena between their buses and prepared to do battle. The traffic on both sides slowed down, appreciative of this impromptu entertainment, while the abandoned passengers crammed to the front of their buses for a better view. But it was far too hot to fight and, sodden and exhausted, the drivers gave up after a few clumsy movements. To the disappointment of the assembled crowd, they were soon returning to their buses and hoicking up their slippery trousers again, defeated by the weather.

At dusk a gust of fresh air sometimes signalled heat's momentary truce before the sweltering night. On the first evening I set off to investigate the streets around our block. Near to our house there was a rotisserie, inside which a vast-bellied man was piling chunks of meat and strings of sausages on to a grill with an expression of weary self-importance. I did not yet know that the *asado*, or barbecue, was an Argentine institution, nor that *asadores*, men who grilled meat, were heroes of the national folklore. Further down the street a patisserie offered a selection of heavy cakes that yearned to be French and, round the next corner, there was an art shop that had a special offer on plaster statuettes of Davids and Virgins, ranged in growing sizes, in the window. There was a bookshop specializing in self-help and inside it a young man, prematurely balding, chewing thoughtfully on his fingernails.

The number of cafés was extraordinary: there was one on the corner of most blocks, and more in between, and they were all full of people. Many of the cafés had very wide sash windows which were flung open to coax in the evening breeze. The customers sat at tables sideways to the windows, with their elbows outside, observing the street scene with a certain superiority. They looked like passengers in the old wooden train compartments, waiting to depart for Patagonia. The wide, open windows produced a strange convergence of street and café. A rich aroma of coffee mingled with the exhaust fumes and the roasting meat; snatches of conversations about family and friends collided with the screech and skid of traffic. Passing by one window I heard a woman say 'Frankly, I'm traumatised.' She stretched the word over five enervated syllables – *trau-ma-ti-za-da* – and I was curious. But a glance at the woman suggested that she was more likely bored than anything else. She was expensively beautiful, and smoking with a languor that gave the lie to trauma.

Everywhere, there was a smell of roasting coffee beans and roasting beef. They were the smells of Buenos Aires.

If you had no guarantor – that is, someone who undertook to pay all your debts, should you abscond – it was almost impossible to get rented accommodation in Buenos Aires. We spent most of the first month trawling through newspapers and meeting estate agents. One of them offered my companion a flat with a nymphomaniac living next door. What better arrangement than to have girlfriend and nymphomaniac under one roof? Another winked and skirted the possibility of a bribe. However, with no guarantee on the table, not even nymphomaniacs and conmen could be persuaded to rent. One night, in desperation, we found ourselves accompanying a Peruvian middleman to the house of a Cuban who sold forged guarantees for 300 dollars apiece. Bearded and smoking a cigar, the man wore an array of badges in support of the Cuban revolution. 'Better be sure you're not yankees,' he warned. 'I have friends who see to it that yankees never have any luck in Buenos Aires.'

I felt sorry for the yankees, but at least we had some luck. Eventually, we managed to secure a flat, without resorting to the Cuban's services, through a complicated network of acquaintances which involved references being sent from London and Jerusalem. The flat was on the fifth and top floor of a slim, nineteenth-century building on the Avenida Córdoba. There was a small kitchen and a bathroom, but otherwise it consisted of one room which had been extended upwards to accommodate two more levels, reached by an industrial iron staircase. The first level was just big enough to support a double bed. The second, which was right inside the building's dome, was little more than a ledge, and a chest of drawers there served also as my desk. From this perch I had a vertiginous view of our sparsely furnished living area below, while through the dome's window I could monitor the encroachment of a new tower block, rising stealthily behind our building.

Our attic flat aspired to studio status, but the bare rafters spoke against such an ambition. For all the effortful rattling of our air-conditioning, the flat baked in the hot weather and we would soon feel it freeze in winter. It was impossible to sleep through the tremendous storms which were periodically whipped up in Patagonia, like rioters, and hounded across the pampa to Buenos Aires. When it was heavy, the rain splashed straight through the roof on to my face as I lay in bed, waking me from jumbled dreams of babies, rats and lifts.

I could stand on a precarious balcony at the front of our building and, seeming to float above six lanes of traffic, feel myself almost obliterated by the noise. Sparkling in the distance to my left were the lights of the Avenida Nueve de Julio. Argentines were proud to call it the widest road in the world and it was murder to cross, sometimes literally. Four blocks away to my right, our avenue met another of the city's main arteries; traffic pushed and jammed its way through this intersection all day and night, to a continuous yowl of horns. Close to that junction was an office block which was undistinguished, except for the fact that the corpse of Eva Perón, 'Evita', had been hidden in an attic there before it was smuggled out of the country in 1957. The man charged with protecting the body went mad with desire for it, and it was said that he had ended his days wandering the streets of Buenos Aires, raving about his lost love. Evita's body, perhaps the best-travelled corpse in history, was rumoured also to have been hidden in various private houses and, for some weeks, behind the screen of a cinema in Palermo. Sometimes

I felt as if Argentina's 'Spiritual Leader' had been hidden all over Buenos Aires; I would come to sense her presence in so many rooms.

The avenue we lived on was lined with apartment blocks and houses of many different styles and sizes, so there were frequent architectural anomalies. Next to our genteel old building towered a modern block that looked like a filing cabinet, out of which each apartment might be pulled by its balcony, its contents examined, then allowed to roll back into place. Further up the road was the magnificent Waterworks, every stone and tile of which had been imported from Britain and France. Flanked by a cordon of palm trees, the Waterworks was a Victorian vision of colonial life in the tropics, and therefore fantastically out of place in Buenos Aires. According to whispered history, Evita had also passed through here on her posthumous wanderings.

A few colonial one-storey houses survived among the city's tower-blocks and often the concrete side of an eighteen-storey building was left naked by its bungalow neighbour. These massive urban canvases were prime sites for political propaganda and pharmaceutical advertisements. Billboards were also dotted along the rooftops: further up our road, a gigantic girl modelling underwear was lit up against the night sky and, facing her, a grinning gaucho held forth a gourd of maté, the national tea: 'It's the taste of Argentina.'

Another balcony at the back of our flat was much quieter, and it was perfect for eavesdropping, since it overlooked an interior space on to which all the other kitchens had windows. Often I sat there among the pot plants listening to shouted snatches of the lives being carried out in the flats below; at meal times the conversations were borne upwards on clouds of roasting beef.

We had four sets of neighbours. José, a retired bank clerk, lived on the first floor with his ninety-five-year-old mother and a mongrel bitch he had found abandoned outside a tango hall. He insulted them noisily and indiscriminately, calling them both 'silly old woman'. He also shouted complaints – about noise – through the ceiling to

Raquel, who lived on the second floor and could sometimes be heard shouting back.

In the mistaken belief that we were aristocratic – he had spotted 'Esq.' on an envelope – José invited us to lunch soon after we moved in. He had made a sort of shepherd's pie in our honour and, as we ate it, he spoke knowledgeably about the history of the British Royal Family, quizzing us on aspects of heraldry and the minutiae of court life. He was evidently surprised that we did not know more and it was when he came to question us on the Knights of the Garter that we discovered his misunderstanding about our origins and tried to make up for it with embarrassed laughter. Sitting at the head of the table, José's tiny mother looked as if she were made of powder balls and might be undone by a gust of wind. She did not speak, except to ask for second helpings and I thought she must be senile. In a patronising way I asked if she was bothered by the noise of traffic, which was much greater on the first floor than at our level. 'I wouldn't be without it now, dear,' she murmured. 'Silence is so overrated.'

José had never fulfilled an ambition to travel beyond the boundaries of Argentina, but he was fascinated by Britain and had read translations of Shakespeare and Wilde. After lunch, as we sat drinking coffee, he described an imaginary walk through central Edinburgh, naming the different streets and monuments with complete accuracy. He even knew some of the paintings to be found in the National Gallery of Scotland, and all this information he gleaned from books. As we were leaving, waiting for the lift to make its rickety descent, José dived back into the sitting room, insisting that I borrow a book; he emerged again with a leather-bound copy of Wilde's *La Importancia de Llamarse Ernesto*. I was moved by José's interest in Britain, and by the courage with which he had faced his life's limitations. Afterwards I wondered if we had been wrong to set him straight on the misunderstanding about our nobility, his disappointment was so tangible, and he had gone to so much trouble with the shepherd's pie.

Raquel, on the second floor, was to become my closest friend.

She was a psychoanalyst, twice divorced, with three grown-up daughters and an eight-year-old son, Santiago. Later I would give English lessons to both mother and son, but, while he progressed well, she was doomed never to master the rudiments. She was adamant that, when more than one person was being greeted, 'hello' should be pluralised to 'hellos'.

Raquel and I saw each other most days and I grew accustomed to her fits of despair about the state of the country. She felt the political scandals and the crises deeply. Sometimes, when the heat was punishing, I found her lying on her bed, the shutters closed and the overhead fan gently ruffling newspapers spread out around her. 'Have you seen this?' she would ask, finding that day's headlined catastrophe without even opening her eyes. 'It's going to get much worse.' At other times, she said, 'If I could just arrange to go to Europe once a year, perhaps I could survive in Argentina.'

On the third floor lived Máximo, an unacknowledged composer who played the piano beautifully, all day and late into the night. His music was often the last thing I heard, clear against the hum of traffic, before I slept. Away from his piano, though, Máximo was invariably overcome with rage. 'Leave this country! Flee!' he used to cry, whenever I came across him waiting for the lift or buying a newspaper from the vendor whose stall was outside our front door. 'Get out of this inferno while you can!'

A homosexual who lived with his mother, Máximo led a life that was practically defined by his loathing of the female neighbours below and above him. He was obsessed by what he saw as their plot to unhinge him. Soon after we moved in he came to our front door to convey, in angry whispers, the importance of thwarting the women at every opportunity. As he catalogued their character defects – they were prostitutes among other things – the colour of Máximo's face rose to match his hair, which had been dyed with henna. His fury centred on the lift. Without consulting him, the neighbours had arranged to have it painted black, with gold touches to match the brass fittings. I liked the decor – the effect was elegant and rather Parisian – but Máximo had wanted the lift painted pale green ('vomit-green', Raquel confided).

Máximo read sinister motives into the women's chosen colour scheme: he thought they wanted to kill him. 'It's oppressive, it's like being in a coffin,' he spluttered to me, whenever I was unfortunate enough to travel upwards with him. Perhaps he knew, as I did, of the statistics concerning fatal accidents in lifts. With a death occurring every two hours, it might be tempting fate to have a lift that already looked like a coffin.

The building's only subdued residents lived on the fourth floor. They were the last surviving relations of a man still widely held to have been the only honest president of the twentieth century. Honesty had rarely been the best policy in Argentina. When this hapless president was overthrown by a military coup, some of his family were murdered, the others went into exile. His nephew, my neighbour, had returned from Italy after the fall of the military junta in 1983. A strange silence reigned on the fourth floor, such that Máximo's piano crescendos cut straight through the space, apparently unmuffled by the presence of people or furniture. But I did sometimes see my neighbour's wife, and I even gave her a few English lessons. She was reading Darwin's *Voyage of the Beagle* and spoke wistfully of European art galleries.

The whole building was permeated with an air of disappointment.

These were bad times in Buenos Aires, but there had been much worse, and one left-wing newspaper existed to remind its readers of that fact. Most days, *Página 12* published a black-and-white snapshot, sometimes several, of men and women. Most of the faces belonged to people in their twenties, neatly groomed and wearing the well-meaning smile people offer to photocabins when they need a passport or a student card. It occurred to me that they glowed with a particular idealism, but perhaps I was too susceptible to hindsight. The poor quality of the prints – they had never been intended as commemorative portraits – bestowed a grainy drama on the images.

These smiling men and women were frozen in time. Their clothes, hairstyles and make-up attached them to an era and a sensibility as surely as those who drowned on the *Titanic* would always be associated with evening gowns and privilege. There was a dramatic name for them too, in fact a new noun had been invented for them. They were known all over the world as 'the disappeared'. They had been tortured and executed by state forces for 'subversive activity'.

Every morning I sat at my desk among the rafters and, distracted from the economy or the latest political scandal, I gazed at these mysterious, smiling youths with a fascination that partly shamed me. Many of them had died at my age, twenty-six, yet I had never felt moved to risk my life for a cause, nor could I imagine what it would be like to be imprisoned and tortured, to meet fear with courage. I scrutinised the gallery of faces for something I could identify as if, by examining them, I might understand something essential about Argentina, and perhaps also about myself.

At the end of the 1960s, a violence had erupted among young Argentines that went beyond the youthful uprisings taking place elsewhere in the world. What seemed at first to be a generational rebellion, directed at the military and moneyed ruling classes, found wider support in a country demoralised by two decades of dictatorship. The 'Montoneros', named after a popular nineteenth-century rebel, were mostly the educated children of middle-class conservatives, but they had rejected their parents' values and turned social activists. Taking their inspiration from Eva Perón, they sought to enact her revolutionary message by blowing up elite country clubs and kidnapping executives, forcing multinationals to make charitable donations or hand out money in shanty towns. In 1970, a group of Montoneros abducted an ex-president, held him ransom for information concerning Evita's missing corpse and, when this was not forthcoming, executed him. From then on, the violence escalated, and soon the government found itself under siege from a number of guerilla groups with different political allegiances – they were Catholics, Marxists and nationalists – but united in one demand: they wanted an exiled leader to return and lead them in socialist revolution. General Perón, discredited and reviled by Argentina's middle classes, was rehabilitated by their children as a hero.

Wealthy on the proceeds of bank-robberies and ransoms, the guerillas were well organised, and motivated by a quasi-religious fanaticism. The forces of law could not contain their violence and finally the anarchy reached such a point that it seemed only one man was capable of restoring order. Yet when the elderly General Perón did return to govern the country in 1973, the violence among different Peronist factions continued, then worsened when he died nine months later, leaving the country in the hands of his inadequate wife, Isabel. A secret death squad was created to fight the guerillas on their own terms, and the monthly toll of murders soared; corpses were left where they fell in the street, or dumped in burning cars on the outskirts of town. By March 1976, one newspaper estimated that a political killing was taking place every five hours, and a bomb attack every three.

The coup, when it came weeks later, was widely welcomed. My newsagent described how, back from honeymoon that very morning, his wife and he had arrived in a city of unrecognisable calm. 'We realised what had happened and thought, "Thank God".' General Videla, described by some as a 'gentleman', was thought to be firm but fair. There would be some restrictions on liberty – that was only to be expected in these desperate circumstances. But he invited the press to be frank, 'not obsequious', and he announced the start of a 'Process of National Reorganisation'. That sounded hopeful: he was going to get the country working again. Argentines welcomed his initiative and looked forward to a return to order after the years of anarchy.

However, Videla's sinister plan, which would become known simply as *el proceso*, was much more ambitious than anyone realised. He had a mission to rid society of its subversives, and a subversive, he explained, was 'anyone who opposes the Argentine way of life'. Equally, a terrorist was 'not just someone with a gun or a bomb, but also someone who spreads ideas that are contrary to Western and

Christian civilisation'. These included liberal opinions on pre-marital sex, divorce and pornography. Under Videla, a new school book advised that women be obedient to their husbands, 'otherwise, anarchy and dissatisfaction become a fact'.

There was no reason for Argentines to be taken unawares, for Videla had made plain his intentions at a press conference in Montevideo, months before the coup. 'In order to guarantee the security of the state,' he had said, 'all the necessary people will die.' Yet most of the population was unaware, for a long time, of the scale of his intent. Even a year after the coup, a poll showed that Argentines largely supported the government.

People started to disappear. They vanished from their homes or from the middle of busy streets. They were taken out of cinemas and shops and hustled into unmarked Ford Falcons in full view of passers-by. Everyone saw what was happening, yet most people found a way to ignore it, for the sake of the peace that had finally been restored to Argentina. The police claimed ignorance, suggesting with smiles to distraught parents that their missing sons and daughters had run away with lovers. The purge was silent and stealthy: there was no longer any evidence of corpses, but everyone saw the Ford Falcons cruising in convoys around the city, carrying gunmen in dark glasses. People justified the disappearance of their neighbours with a now infamous phrase: 'There must be some reason for it.'

'We were sleepwalkers,' one man, shaking his head sadly, told me. 'We did not want to know; perhaps we still do not want to know.'

Videla's 'purification' of Argentina was to involve hundreds of servicemen, policemen and doctors in an act of mass abduction and murder. Public servants would learn to become torturers. Yet the supposed target of the *proceso*, the guerillas, accounted for only about 20 per cent of those who were killed. Some of them died in shoot-outs, or took cyanide to cheat the interrogators. Others were kept alive and later freed, and some of them ended up working for the government, or even for the sort of lucrative company they had once attacked. It was easy for them to dismiss their past activism as youthful excess: they had survived, after all.

But no one knew for sure how many people had died. The National Commission on the Disappeared, CONADEP, set up in 1983 by the new, democratically elected government to investigate and document the practices of *el proceso*, registered 8,960 cases. However, there were reckoned to be thousands more people who, through fear or shame, never came forward to denounce the murder of relations and loved ones. During the dictatorship it had been dangerous to confess that a member of your family had disappeared, and some parents had even disowned the children whose politics and behaviour they found troublesome. Where whole families had disappeared, there was no one to register the deaths with CONADEP. Human rights groups believed that the true number of disappeared was closer to 20,000 or even 30,000. It was ironic that, in a country where you could be arrested for not carrying an identity card, so many people were now unaccounted for, so many thousands of identities were in limbo.

The guerillas' vicious campaign, which had taken several hundred lives, provoked an extreme and disproportionate revenge. Among the disappeared were children, adolescents and pensioners, but the vast majority of the state's victims were educated, politically aware men and women between the ages of twenty and thirty-five. They were intellectuals, professionals and factory workers; they were doctors who worked in shanty towns, psychoanalysts and sociologists. Many were students of politics or literature, 'café revolutionaries' who – like their peers all over the world – had posters of Che Guevara on their walls. Some of them were involved in community projects, some had written idealistic poetry, or espoused the freedoms claimed by French students rioting in 1968. Others had no interest in politics or ideals at all but were unfortunate enough to have the wrong friends or the wrong surname, or to be turning the wrong street corner when a Ford Falcon passed. Even intellectual curiosity was subversion enough to merit death. The Governor of Buenos Aires, General Ibérico St Jean, warned that it was not enough to stand on the sidelines if you wanted to save your life. 'First we shall kill all the subversives,' he promised, 'then we shall kill their collaborators; then ... their sympathisers, then ... those who remain indifferent; and finally we shall kill the timid.' One young doctor, tortured for months before he was allowed to go free, was told that he was being punished for his 'goody-goody' work with the underprivileged.

For the span of a decade, Argentina must have been delirious with self-hatred. How else can one explain the fanatical persecution of people whose only crime, sometimes, was to have read the wrong books? They were murdered, these smiling men and women, not by a foreign army, but by the authority of their own country. Denied a trial, they were tortured to death, sometimes over many months. Thousands were dropped into the River Plata from planes or dumped in communal graves. Their families were rarely notified of their deaths, or even of their resting places. Some of the texts alongside the snapshots in *Página 12* still demanded 'Where is he?' or 'Let her reappear alive.' There was a slogan that adorned most of these memorials: 'We won't forgive or forget.'

When General Galtieri took charge of the junta in 1981, the worst of the terror was over, and the dictatorship finally ended in humiliation, after the 1982 Falklands War. By the time I arrived in Argentina, the country had celebrated the tenth anniversary of its new democracy. There had been two free elections, Hyperinflation – which had reached 5,000 per cent in the late 1980s – had been brought under control by a plan to tag the local currency, the peso, to the dollar. The army had been trimmed and tamed to the point where it would never again be able to mount a successful coup.

Democracy was in place but, as the political analysts often said, a 'democratic culture' had yet to be created. This was a problem common to all post-dictatorships: it would take at least a generation for people to understand their new freedom and responsibilities. But there was a particular sense of unease in Argentina. The worst excesses of *el proceso* were only fifteen years off, yet they were rarely mentioned. The country seemed to suffer like an amnesiac who knows that something terrible has happened, but cannot fathom the extent of the atrocity. The tragedies of the last two decades were over, but there was a widespread feeling that they had not properly been dealt with by the national conscience.

Trials for war crimes had been held, but in 1990, with a restless army threatening coups, President Menem had decreed a general amnesty for all the guerillas, torturers, army chiefs and the three dictators who had been imprisoned. Argentina should forget about the past, he had said, and reclaim the future.

If the amnesty was necessary to safeguard Argentina's democracy, many thought it meant that the damage done to the nation could not now be resolved. The upshot, they said, was a 'culture of silence', which had robbed Argentina of its right to grieve and encouraged bitterness and anxiety. Knowing that one-time torturers and assassins were at large and unpunished terrified even those who had not experienced *la represión* at first hand. There was a continuing debate, periodically taken up by newspapers, television and cultural centres, about the best way to treat the past. Should it be left to slip away, as the president advised, or should it be confronted, however painful the consequences? Young Germans learned about the Holocaust. What would Argentine children be taught about their history?

The Buenos Aires I first encountered in 1993 was trying to resolve these painful dilemmas. It was a city that was beginning to rediscover the culture and sophistication that had once made it such a fashionable destination. New shopping malls were opening and the opera house was once more playing host to international stars. But it was also a city where some of the world's most evil men walked free. The tortured feared daily the possibility of meeting their torturers. The concentration camps where thousands had lost their lives still stood, not one of them marked by so much as a plaque. It was, in a sense, a country in a crucible. Argentina had been violated, but the violators were not going to be punished. The tragedy of what had happened seemed to swim in the afternoon heat.

CHAPTER TWO

Crossed Wires

TOO OFTEN, OUR mornings began with an early telephone call, sending one of us stumbling down the perilous iron stairs. The voices on the other end of the line varied, but the intonation was always elderly and somehow reedy and querulous. The question was always the same.

'Doctor?'

'I'm sorry, you've got the wrong number.' This was a formula I could repeat almost without waking up.

'This isn't the surgery, then?'

As far as we knew, no doctor had ever worked in our flat – one could hardly imagine a less suitable venue for a surgery. But the elderly callers kept on calling and often they were argumentative and even rude. They must have thought that I was an over-protective receptionist, or even that I was a doctor myself, shirking patients. Some of the callers slammed the telephone down on me and at least one woman called me an *imbécil*.

I could never lose the habit of courtesy on the telephone. 'Perhaps there's a misprint in the telephone directory,' I suggested to one, 'maybe the operator can help you.'

The voice at the other end registered ancient alarm. 'I don't need an operation, stupid girl! I'm just not feeling very well!'

Argentina's telephone system was newly privatised, but still it was unreliable, and about half of the calls that reached our house every day were intended for someone else. Sometimes, the number that had been dialled differed in every single digit from ours and there was nothing for the caller to do but to keep trying to get through, to their mounting annoyance and ours. I played go-between for one woman and her ailing mother whose attempts to communicate always landed up at our house. After this had happened several times we struck up a deal: when they wanted to speak, I left my handset off the hook for a few seconds – it was the only way their connection would work.

Misdirected callers rarely bothered to conceal their exasperation on reaching our number. 'Who are *you*?' the anonymous voices demanded, or even 'Who the *hell* are you?' Once I had confessed, stammering, to the wrong name, they usually hung up without ceremony. However, a few stayed on line, their curiosity piqued by my foreign-sounding name and accent. Where are you from? callers asked. Why are you here? Well fancy wanting to come to Argentina! What do you think of our country? On hearing that I was English, people often wanted to ask me about the famous 'London smog'. And what did I think would happen to the Royal Family? Was I for Charles or Diana?

The regime of crossed lines forced on me a new understanding of the frailty of communication. I had the sensation, not necessarily unpleasant, of taking part in a massive game of Blind Man's Buff. One made calls into the void, with no certain idea who would answer them. Equally, when the telephone rang in our house, there was no knowing who would be on the other end of line. It might be a friend or a stranger, a news editor from London, or one of the villains the city graffiti railed against. Sometimes I anticipated a husky voice insinuating violence – journalists often received death threats in Buenos Aires.

The misconnections could also prove useful. A translator took advantage of one crossed line to ask me for a definition of 'hurly-burly' and on another I found a tango instructor, offering competitive rates. A man who could not reach his girlfriend asked *me* on a date, instead. One time, I rang an economist to arrange an interview and his female neighbour also came on the line. They had previously only ever exchanged greetings in the corridor but now, on my telephone bill, they struck up a giggling rapport, and agreed to meet for coffee. In the excitement of this new encounter, my interview request fell by the wayside.

Somewhere, the Argentine operators must have been weeping with laughter at the disruption they oversaw. From time to time the telephones rang in two houses simultaneously, joining in a brief, resentful union people who would normally never dream of contacting one another. For months I would answer the telephone, wrenched from sleep, from the shower or from cooking a meal, to find myself listening to Scott Joplin's 'The Entertainer', on a repeating loop. Irritation finally determined me to find out who my tormentor was and, at the end of eight 'Entertainers', I found myself connected to a voice one could well imagine might belong to a Joplin fan.

'Southside Mechanics,' murmured the voice.

'Fix your phone or change the bloody music!' I shouted before hanging up. I felt better for shouting, and then immediately worse – after all, it was not the mechanic's fault, but the system's, and I was beginning to sound like one of the lunatic pensioners who rang every morning.

The best crossed lines offered a glimpse into an anonymous life, randomly selected from the millions in Buenos Aires, complete with its incumbent secrets and woes. When I was really lucky, the ringing telephone summoned me to eavesdrop on secret conversations; I would pick up the handset to hear two voices already on the line.

'If you really can't . . .' a woman's voice, discreetly manipulative.

'Well, I suppose I *could*' – his emphasis filled the word with sex – 'if I left work early and told her I was going to my analyst. I could be with you by seven o'clock.'

'*Mi amor*, that's *three hours* away.'

The improving service slightly reduced the number of crossed lines, although the pensioners stubbornly kept up their early-morning harassment. Then, finally, we bought a cordless telephone and there was a new potential for confusion. Our telephone used the same frequency as Máximo's, which meant that our conversations were habitually infiltrated by him, ranting about the lift and the treachery of women to his friends. It was strange to find my conversations to British and American editors, which were difficult at the best of times, interrupted by Máximo's hysterical lamentations. Then again the rest of the world was beginning to seem so far away, sometimes I wondered if anything outside Buenos Aires really existed.

A large city has a tempo, a rhythm with which the new arrival seeks to fall in step – but I could not gauge the rhythm of Buenos Aires. It seemed that there was no particular time at which people awoke, went to work, lunched, returned home, went to bed. Trying to reach someone at the office was a wasted effort. Invariably, the person you were looking for had not yet arrived and no one knew when he was due in. No matter what day it was, the advice was to 'ring back on Monday'. It took me several weeks to see that this was a stalling device: Monday was a fiction.

Only gradually did I come to realise that life in Buenos Aires could not be subdued and contained by timetables – even if you set off with the best intentions, each day held in store its quota of disruptions. Meetings were habitually late, cancelled or skipped. At the supermarket varieties of produce disappeared from the shelves, or shot up in price, because of disputes in the provinces. Plays and lectures started late, because everyone, including the performers, was behind schedule. In addition to the public holidays celebrating the Argentine Flag, the Argentine Race and, of course, Argentina's right to the Malvinas, there were special days in the year to honour journalists, accountants, lawyers and secretaries; students, lovers, housewives and friends – all providing marvellous excuses to take more time off work. Our local laundrette made posters and put out a tipping box, in anticipation of Launderer's Day.

Each new day unwound a unique set of problems, some of them serious. At any time and without explanation, you might lose your telephone line, your electricity or your water supply, perhaps for several weeks. Say, having been deprived of that essential service, you were then charged for it, and found yourself taking time off work to remonstrate at the offices of whichever company it was that had ruined your day. After queuing for an hour or so, your complaint would be heard by a disdainful and disbelieving clerk, usually through a screen of cigarette smoke. You might have to return and complain several times more, to different bureaucrats, perhaps making veiled threats or dropping the names of powerful friends, before anything was done to remedy the situation. By then you might have lost several days' work and contracted urban stress. A premature death was surely on the cards.

Bureaucrats were a species I had never really encountered before, except in Russian literature, but now, with so much complaining to be done, they became an inevitable feature of my life. I found I had hours to study these dour-faced men and women as they smoked, made phone calls and typed with just two fingers on very old manual typewriters. I came to know very well the typical bureaucrat's office, adorned by a framed photograph of the president and sometimes an Argentine flag, flagging. What air there was in these windowless offices hung heavy with smoke and abandoned hope; the overhead fan, casting shadowy carousels on the walls, was powerless to budge it. Occasionally the atmosphere was cleared by an eruption of fury from the ranks of queuers, but this was rare – the majority of people accepted their wait with a blank resilience. They waited and smoked, waited and fanned themselves with bureaucratic forms, and commented to their neighbours that that was the only thing such forms were good for. A ruined day in Buenos Aires had a horrid tendency to become a ruined week or month. Whole years, whole lives could be wrecked by the 'system'. No wonder sales of sedatives and anti-depressants were rocketing.

I wondered, as I queued, if Argentine bureaucrats had always been unhelpful, or if they started their careers with enthusiasm and energy and were steadily disillusioned. Perhaps there was a moment in the youth of a clerk when she realised how slim the chances were of a life beyond this office – exotic holidays and dizzy promotions would never come her way, no Hollywood star would want to rescue her from this grim shuffling of papers and people – and the gloom set in there. In such a moment of realisation a face might well begin to fall, and, with the successive years of disappointment, creep further towards the ground. It occurred to me then that the two-fingered typing must be a weapon of revenge, designed to sap the determination of those people who still had the energy to complain.

At night, on television, we saw stories of people's lives thrown into tumult for a nonsense. Sometimes the images were so violent that it was my instinct to laugh. The bloody victims of machete attacks were interviewed as they lay on their stretchers, *en route* to the ambulance (the paramedics actually slowed down for the cameras). Police were shown beating up immigrant squatters. A woman, hysterical, screamed 'Where's the justice?' outside a courtroom.

Once, after a bad flood which put out half the city's lights, a small boy was swept off the street into an open sewer. His father was shown on television, vainly searching the neighbourhood's sewerage for his child's body. The emergency services had been called, but they never arrived, 'perhaps because we are poor', the man suggested, without sarcasm.

Following the drama with relish, every evening's bulletin hunted down the man in some sewer or other. 'Have you found your son yet?' a malicious journalist asked him. Each time he politely replied that he had not, but that he would keep looking. The authorities' lack of accountability was never probed. There was no call for an inquiry, no outraged comment in the press. I realised, from this and other similar episodes, that people did not expect to be served by the government they had elected and paid for. The concept of the state having a duty to help and protect its citizens was recognisable from American films, but no one seriously expected it to apply to Argentina. My occasional suggestions that it ought to were met with gales of laughter from my friends. Argentina – they pointed out with rueful smiles – had one of the most noble, enlightened constitutions in the world, but what good were words on paper?

'Your problem', said Raquel, 'is that you try to see Argentina as a normal country. It's abnormal. It's a country that doesn't work.'

There was, at least, a freedom to complain. Demonstrations were frequent, fervent, and sometimes the whole city was encouraged to take part in them, with radio announcements and scattered leaflets urging a mass show of solidarity at an appointed hour. One evening, thousands of *porteños* appeared on their balconies, banging saucepans with wooden spoons to protest against government corruption; another time they kept a minute's silence in memory of a murdered journalist. When the cost of local calls doubled, people boycotted the telephone for a fixed number of hours a day. With so many protests, it was hard to remember when to keep silent and when to be noisy, when to light candles and when to boycott the telephone – assuming it was working.

On Thursday afternoons, the Mothers of the Disappeared held a vigil in front of the president's palace in the Plaza de Mayo, to protest the continuing freedom of their children's killers. On Wednesdays it was the turn of a more violent and noisy faction: the elderly. Under the new economic regime, pensioners had lost almost all entitlement to state benefits – their money had simply evaporated during the days of hyperinflation. The situation was so dire that television channels all featured a 'pensioners' corner', a daily bulletin explaining the government's complex proposals to make up for the loss of pensions with bonds redeemable at a later date. On Wednesday afternoons, thousands of pensioners held an enraged demonstration outside the Congress, which was liable to end in a riot. They were a bizarre sight, these geriatric hooligans, rattling crash barriers and spraying graffiti; one old man could do a trick with his false teeth for the cameras. Once, during a protest a septuagenarian activist had her wig stolen by a rival group of pensioners. Infuriated, she ran squawking through the streets around the Congress. Her legs swathed in support bandages, her earrings an obscene adornment to her baldness, she looked remarkably like a dodo.

The rhythmic beating of a bombo drum, signalling another protest, became a peculiarly violent sound to my ears. Sometimes I heard the distant drums from my perch in the dome and felt the skin tighten on my neck. I would go down and stand on the front balcony as the people streamed underneath, a dizzying turbulence of banners, fliers and colours. There were protests against corruption in politics and the law courts, against the government's economic policy and university underfunding. On the anniversary of the Falklands War, a noisy procession of veterans made its way to the war monument, vowing to return and recapture the islands.

Once, coming out of a back street on to our avenue, I found myself swept into a Peronist rally campaigning for the re-election of the president. The noise and movement were tremendous; the demonstrators blew whistles and waved Argentine flags and there was the violent thrashing of the drum again, very loud this time, because I was right beside it. The drummer's face, red from exertion and pouring sweat, was a picture of derangement; his features seemed contorted by a painful ecstasy. He was beating the drum with such a frenzy that he had scraped his knuckles raw, and the parchment was streaming with blood. Yet still he went on, bashing the bleeding hand against the drum. I thought the man was crazed in the pursuit of politics; either that, or he was a slave to the drum. In any case, I could never forget him and his derangement. A long time afterwards, when I was living in London, the rhythmic banging of bass-heavy music from a passing car could still induce in me a momentary anxiety I recognised from those times. For a few seconds I could feel transported to the streets of Buenos Aires.

To the concept of the 'fictional Monday', I soon added that of the 'missing key', because it turned out that keys, or rather the absence of them, played a crucial role in the daily life of the capital. During the course of researching articles, I was often told that I could not do something because 'the person with the key has not come in'. This enigmatic excuse was used to deflect a range of quite different requests.

One afternoon, not long after I had arrived in Buenos Aires, I asked an employee at one of the libraries if I could have an article photocopied. 'That won't be possible,' she said, regretfully. 'The person who works the photocopier is not available.'

'When will he be available?'

'I don't know. You could try coming back on Monday.'

My heart sank at the mention of Monday. I needed the article for work I was doing now. I was reluctant to copy the whole thing out and, anyway, why should I, when there was a machine to do it for me? Making photocopies had previously seemed a simple business, but now I saw it for the delicate enterprise it really was. Behind the librarian, the photocopier took on the guise of a brooding animal that could be understood and tamed only by one master, a man so special that it was impossible to know when he might next be available. I pictured myself returning every Monday, perhaps for the rest of my life, in the hope of finding him. 'Maybe you could make the copy for me,' I ventured, 'or I could make it myself.'

'No, I'm not authorised to do that,' the woman insisted. 'Besides, I don't have the key to the cupboard where the paper for the photocopier is kept.'

'I have some paper of my own that would do.'

The woman's features hardened and it was possible to see her resolve stiffening into something almost sinister – a deliberate attempt to frustrate. Her determination not to be seen as subservient had evidently now become a badge of honour. The photocopier, tantalisingly close, winked little red and green eyes at me; it seemed to murmur imprecations. I was damned if I would go all the way back home without the information I needed and, for some mysterious reason, probably buried in history, the librarian was damned if she would help. I saw that we were locked in a struggle to which the key was not currently available. 'Come back on Monday,' the librarian enunciated, bitterly.

But I knew about Mondays by now, and I was beginning to know about threats too. I decided, for the first time, to try one out.

'I am a foreign journalist,' I said carefully. 'I am going to see your president and I need a copy of this article straightaway.'

There was a second's tension between us, then the librarian grimaced: she recognised my trump. Scowling, she snatched away the article, went to the photocopier and adeptly made a copy of it. The process took about thirty seconds. She overcharged me for it, but that was to be expected.

As for me, I had learned the first important lesson of life in Buenos Aires: *viveza criolla*, or 'creole cunning'. Argentines held it to be a national characteristic, of which some were proud and others ashamed. It might loosely be defined as artful lying or cheating. Diego Maradona, the country's great footballing idol, was, somebody told me, the supreme embodiment of *viveza criolla*.

Porteños understood each day's scope for disruption, and the clever ones knew how to exploit it for their own ends. I learned early on that contacts were everything. Raquel introduced me to her bank manager, her hairdresser and one or two shop assistants, instructing them to give me preferential treatment. Each of them kissed me and promised to be helpful, though I was nervous of the hairdresser, who was named after one of Argentina's bloodiest dictators. Raquel said she could set me up with a reliable but inexpensive doctor and she revealed her secret for skipping the queue at her bank, which was always to go with a bag of croissants, enough for all the bank staff. 'I probably spend more on bribes than I earn in interest on my savings account,' she admitted, but at least the outlay guaranteed her swift and friendly service. Sometimes the bank manager even left his office to greet her, embracing her warmly. The croissants came from one of the best bakeries in Buenos Aires.

Such a strategy was vital because otherwise the greater part of every day might be spent in queues of one sort or another. All bills had to be paid in person, and the payment of just one could sometimes take more than an hour. The premises of banks, utilities and services often had queues snaking out of them and around the block. Yet inside, behind the counters, girls in mini-skirts could be seen filing their nails or giggling on the telephone. The sight of dozens of people waiting to be served, far from galvanising the employees to work, was possibly the source of a sadistic ego-boost. If people had to queue for your services, then you must be very important. If you had no queue, but the bank next door did, that was a bad sign, it showed that you were not in demand. The wealthy had servants to stand in queues for them and large companies employed young men and women simply for this purpose. Everybody else had to take time off work to pay their bills, which was one of the reasons they were never in the office when I telephoned.

There was an expression I heard people use during the hours spent waiting in queues: *Buenos Aires me mata*, 'Buenos Aires is killing me.' It had originally been the title of a column in one of the newspapers, then of a cabaret show, but now people could be heard saying it all the time, sometimes in the form of a wry joke, accompanied by a shrug. At other times the sentiment seemed more serious, as if people really felt that the city itself, even emptied of its people, could have a malevolent purpose all of its own, as if the very architecture had a secret mission to oppress and defeat its inhabitants.

I may have intimidated the librarian in order to get my photocopy, but, strictly speaking, I had not lied. I *was* going to see the president. Raquel had invited me to attend the first night of the Buenos Aires Book Fair, one of the cultural highlights of the year, which was to be inaugurated by the president, with many local celebrities in attendance. I had no choice but to accompany her in perfumed tights.

That morning I had nipped out to buy a pair, not yet having learned that in Argentina nothing could be nipped out for; even fast food was slow. I had ended up in a special hosiery boutique looking on as a beautiful and disdainful woman produced individual pairs of tights in different shades and deniers from tiny drawers. The tights were expensive and they were already leg-shaped, which I found a fascinating novelty, but when I got my pair out of the packet at home, they exuded a forceful scent of Parma violets. There was nothing to be done about it now; I resigned myself to an evening spent apologising for my legs.

In the event, Raquel was comprehensively perfumed herself and so was the taxi driver; I thought that my legs' whiff would probably not rise above the mélange of aromas as we drove towards the site of the Book Fair. It had taken us twenty minutes to get a taxi. The roads were packed at that time of the evening, and taxis, which were cheap, were in demand. To complicate matters, several sets of traffic lights were on the blink and circulation had been hindered by a protest in the afternoon.

'Driving in Buenos Aires is like playing Russian Roulette,' said the taxi driver softly, as if he foresaw his own death on one of these hazardous intersections. His face was thin and lined and his air of melancholy was enhanced most effectively by the tangos wafting from the car radio. Argentina's twenty-four-hour tango station, FM Tango, was started at the instigation of General Perón, who passed a decree to safeguard the amount of 'national' music played on radio stations. Tangos were disapproved of by high society – and, since Perón disapproved of high society, he tormented them with tangos. With its memories of lost homelands and cruel girlfriends, its pre-occupation with suicide, the genre could be excessively sad. A previous military government had instructed composers to curb their misery, but there was no market for lively tangos. Above the clamour of my legs, Raquel's hair and the taxi driver's chest rose the perfumed suffering of Argentina's national music.

> That ermine coat I gave you,
> all lined in gold lamé,
> which used to keep you warm

> when you came out of the cabaret,
> has turned out in the end to be more
> lasting than your love,
> your passion's died already
> and I'm still paying for the coat.

'Nothing's changed,' sighed Raquel. 'I have to buy everything in quotas.' She was fifty and very attractive, with shoulder-length brown hair and green eyes. Raquel's divorces made her seem glamorous, and she was wearing a pale pink mini-skirt and a matching jacket that emphasised her long brown legs, but she was friendly and instinctively I liked her. In the intimacy of the taxi we started to *tutear* one another, to use the informal 'you'. Raquel told me that she knew Argentina's president, Dr Carlos Menem. She was confident that he would come to greet us at the Book Fair.

'I knew him fifteen years ago, when he was governor of La Rioja. He had sideboards then and he used to wear Oxfords and a poncho.' Raquel roared with laughter and I laughed with her, though I only found out later that 'Oxfords' were flares. 'You wouldn't catch him dead in a poncho now,' she said.

Even by Latin American standards, Argentina's president was flamboyant. Soon after taking office, he had commanded headlines when, irritated by his wife, he had an army officer forcibly remove her from the presidential palace. Asked on a television show if he would loan his wife for a million dollars, like the hero of the film *Indecent Proposal*, the president had said, 'I'm quite happy to give her away.' Señora Menem retaliated with regular, tearful interviews, in which she vowed to win back her husband, who she said had been spoilt by power and fame.

The president's family enjoyed a lifestyle extravagant far beyond most Argentines' dreams and well outstripping the means of his own salary. Every month they spent thousands of dollars on jewels, clothes and cosmetic operations – for they were very vain. Dr Menem refused to admit to his own face-lift, causing great public hilarity when he dismissed the tell-tale bruising as 'a wasp sting'. The premier's celebrated tussles with his hair held the nation in thrall; one daily political cartoon featured, as a separate character, the presidential hairpiece. The site of some of these struggles was a hair salon specially built aboard the president's private jet; Dr Menem rarely went anywhere without a hairdresser.

Argentina's president adored celebrity. Often he was seen on the society pages dancing tangos with beautiful young actresses – he had no qualms about cancelling political commitments if an international 'supermodel' was in town, and available to be lunched. A raggle-taggle series of fading American and European filmstars attended barbecues at the palace. Sometimes one saw photographs of one-time starlets, just recognisable from 1970s television thrillers, peering at plates of grilled sausages with a look of bewilderment, as if wondering why middle age and oblivion should be a route to friendship with the president of a South American republic.

Polls suggested that most Argentines deplored their president's lifestyle, and that they were nervous of his authoritarianism – not since General Perón had a leader wielded so much power. Dr Menem had such a penchant for decrees that he even considered issuing one to save his favourite football team from relegation. The most pressing national concern was no longer hyperinflation, but 'hyperpresidentialism'. Yet most people felt that Dr Menem represented Argentina's best chance of making up for half a century lost to corruption, inefficiency and dictatorship. He had neatly subverted the national obsession with Peronism by campaigning on a Peronist, populist ticket, only to change tactics immediately he got into office, with a sweeping round of privatisations and cost-cutting. Everyone agreed that this was a devious trick, but they could also admire it as a great example of *viveza criolla*. Besides, the deception seemed to be paying off: after years of spiralling hyperinflation. Argentina's economy had stabilised and was growing.

At the same time, the cost of living had soared, and with it unemployment. Among the middle classes it was now common to juggle two or more jobs. Taxi drivers often revealed themselves to be out-of-work engineers or civil servants. I knew a foreign editor who also worked for an advertising agency, then took a third job at the weekend. Even then, he told me, his suits were borrowed. Times were hard and Dr Menem made no promise that they would get better soon. He referred to his government's stringent economic measures as 'surgery without anaesthetic'.

By the time we pulled up in front of the Book Fair, crowds of photographers and security guards were already milling around outside in anticipation of the president's arrival. Raquel put an immaculately manicured hand on my arm. 'When he kisses you, be careful not to touch his hair,' she said. 'Part of it is false and could come off.' Inside the building, she pulled me through the crush of people in the foyer to the barrier. I was anxious now about the imminent kiss, and the danger of dislodging the president's toupée.

'He should see us here,' she said. 'He's due any minute.'

In fact, we waited nearly an hour in the crush before a battery of flashlights outside announced the tardy arrival of Argentina's leader. At that moment the crowd behind us lunged forward, pushing us against the barrier. There was a struggle as reporters were jostled to one side by guards, then the president entered. A surprisingly small, tanned man, with hair that glittered suspiciously, he stood in the foyer, smiled briefly and was promptly borne upstairs by the meaty brigade of security men.

Everyone who had been waiting in the foyer – perhaps all of us expecting to be kissed – now stampeded next door, into a hall the size of an airport hangar, where about a thousand people had been waiting among the book stalls for the president to arrive. Some people were asleep in their chairs, others were leafing through the books on display at hundreds of stalls. Books about corruption dominated the bestseller lists, reflecting Argentines' present concern, but American self-help was also very popular, and the British Royal Family was catching on.

Smiling and waving, President Menem appeared on a balcony at the front of the hall, with flunkeys, a bishop and several beautiful girls. A plaintive fanfare arose from the military brass band, which was symbolically distant on a balcony at the far end of the hall. Until 1983, the army's job had been to search the stalls at the Book Fair every year, for subversive or immoral material, paying particular attention to imported books, and atlases that made mention of the Falkland Islands, rather than Las Islas Malvinas. Now its much diminished role was to provide a rendition of the national anthem – one that was, possibly deliberately, tuneless. We all rose to sing it anyway. We all swore, three times, to die gloriously.

After the last rousing deathwish, officials started stepping forward, one by one, to make speeches about books and the president's attachment to them. One bade us picture the truckloads of schoolbooks that were even now being dispatched to the furthest reaches of Patagonia. Publishers were thriving as never before, he said; the National Library had been completed after twenty-five years of stalling bureaucracy. All this was thanks to the president.

Up on the balcony the girls clapped and smiled. The president's hair glittered immodestly.

The speeches were very long, and during their course many of those lucky enough to have found a seat joined the ranks of the sleeping, while others browsed surreptitiously among the biographies of British royals.

Finally the beautiful girls began to droop. The present speaker was straining to make a link between the president's devotion to great literature and his commitment to democracy and freedom of expression. A man standing beside me snorted and whispered under his breath, 'Great literature? He'd swap the complete works of Borges for a spin in a Ferrari any day.'

Then the bishop was called upon to bless the books – the most stringent precaution the government would take against immorality in books nowadays. He looked anxious and frail, as if worried for his job. Scattering droplets of water, he painted a sign of the cross in the air, and there was a fluttering of hands across the hall, as thousands of people crossed themselves. From the back balcony came a tuneless military fanfare.

'Let there be light,' the bishop intoned, carefully.

And finally the president himself stepped forward. There was a ripple of anticipation. Those who were still awake roused the sleeping, while others left off their browsing and moved to get a better view. The president flung open his arms to the assembled crowd and cried.

'Brothers! Sisters! Book lovers! I embrace you to my heart!'

'Viva el presidente!' cried a voice at the back of the hall. 'Viva la República Argentina!'

At night I stood on the front balcony, the lights flickering in thousands of homes around me, and watched the traffic streaming up the road away from the city centre and towards the pampa. In the café opposite, the young men who played chess for hours on end reluctantly packed away their queens and castles. The giant underwear model smiled from her rooftop at the stars. I pondered the suggestive murmurings I had heard on the crossed line and wondered where in the capital that secret adultery had taken place and what would be its outcome. What had the economist and his neighbour got up to after their coffee date? How many relationships had been lost and found on the telephone that day? From one of the illuminated windows opposite, a woman's scream flew into the air: 'I said I'm sick and tired of all this.'

Jorge Luis Borges, Argentina's most celebrated writer, loved Buenos Aires; when he talked about the south, he meant the south of Buenos Aires. Friends recalled how he had walked through the city obsessively at night, 'feeling' it, later to transcribe the pattern of streets into fabulous stories of labyrinths and invented universes.

It was said that Borges had died out of devotion for his city – but then he invented Buenos Aires anew in his poems and short stories. In his mind it was a mythological place, populated by the ghosts of war heroes, of swaggering knife-fighters and tango dancers. 'I cannot believe that Buenos Aires had a start,' he wrote. 'She seems as eternal to me as air and water.' And at night Borges imagined this dream of a city to become tenuous, imperilled.

> there's a moment
> in which the city's existence is at the brink of danger and disorder
> and that is the trembling moment of dawn
> when those who are dreaming the world are few
> and only a handful of night owls preserve
> ashen and sketchy
> a vision of the streets
> which they will afterward define for others.
> The hour in which the persistent dream of life
> is in danger of breaking down,
> the hour in which God might easily
> destroy all his work!

'Lots of words are spelt differently in the United States,' Santiago told me, during one of our English lessons. 'For instance, the Americans spell "night", "nite".'

'Not officially,' I said. 'That's a kind of slang. When they spell it "nite" it's because they want to say something special about the night.'

Santiago looked blank. 'What do they want to say?'

'It's a sort of joke,' I said. 'They're making out that night-time is fun.'

'It's not a good joke,' said Santiago, truthfully.

Very late at night, when the illuminated windows were few and the traffic reduced to a pack of prowling taxis, poor families from the shanty towns took over Buenos Aires for a few hours. Silently they swept through the streets, sorting through rubbish bags and collecting discarded fruit and vegetables from outside the super-markets. Some people left clothes and toys outside with the bags, knowing that these would have vanished long before the rubbish collectors made their early-morning rounds. It was a neat, anony-mous transaction, with no embarrassment to either party. The city at night was the guilty conscience of the day. Out came the poor, the despairing, the graffitists with their urgent evocations of Evita and Perón.

Once, returning late from a friend's house, we came across the body of a man who, perhaps only minutes before, had killed himself by jumping from a balcony into the street. He lay naked on the ground under a skimpy blanket which the attendant policemen had arranged across his lower back. The man's hands were pressed together under his body, as if he had dived into the night.

I could not get to sleep after that and for ages I moved uncomfortably around the bed, thinking about the dead man. It was hot, but the power had been cut off that evening so there was no relief to be had from a shower or the air-conditioning. A mosquito, threatening from the rafters, obliged me to pull the sheet over my head, in spite of the heat.

I must finally have found sleep, because some time during the night I was jolted awake, my heart pounding, by a bolt of noise and bright lights. In the moment's disorientation I imagined a police raid: I thought I heard footsteps on the marble stairs and a Ford Falcon purring in the street outside. But it was simply that the electricity had been reinstated, the fridge, the lift and air-conditioning had set about their work with renewed vigour. Here was cool air just when I had managed to do without it; water when I no longer needed it; bright lights when I craved darkness.

CHAPTER THREE

A Nation on the Couch

ORTH AND SOUTH, there were riots. Our television showed scenes of burning buildings, of men's faces gaping with rage. The sources of discontent, as usual, were corruption and bad administration. Several regional governments had exhausted their budgets and the Treasury was no longer prepared to bail them out, so thousands of public workers had not been paid for months. Argentina's worst-run provinces were little better than fiefdoms, with top jobs awarded to the governor's friends and family and corruption absorbing the better part of federal funds. Crimes that implicated members of the political families had a habit of going uninvestigated, there were countless stories of bribery and extortion. Now the masses were taking their revenge by laying siege to the government buildings and setting them alight.

At night I lay in bed and strained to hear the roar of looting taking place thousands of miles away across the pampa. Storms were a frequent obstacle to sleep, and it was easy to conjure approaching drums and the clatter of overturned cars out of the thunderclaps. I wondered, with a curiosity, if the distant insurrections might reach the capital. An elderly woman I met at a friend's tea party evoked the 1940s, when upper-class *porteños* feared an invasion of the *desca-*

misados or 'shirtless ones', the provincial poor. 'We lived in terror. We thought the end was coming.' Her face, like an old cloth bag with a little clasp for lips, shut tight in contempt. 'We thought there would be an infestation of the working classes.'

So, there were riots on the pampa and demonstrations in Buenos Aires, and in our kitchen a steady column of ants paraded across the walls, through the cupboards and back out on to the balcony, laden with booty. In idle moments I watched them processing back to camp with a miniature inventory of our last meal: tiny crumbs of bread and cheese, specks of peanut. I reasoned that they were performing a valuable service; I would rather have ants than cock-roaches. But our new neighbour spoke of an infestation. 'We should zap them before it gets worse,' he suggested.

The neighbour's name was Gabriel; he was thirty, and a narcissist. He paid a token rent for the room next to our flat on the fifth floor, which had originally been intended as a place to store cleaning implements and for a concierge to sit during the day. The neighbours had long ago dispensed with the services of their concierge, who was, they said, expensive and lazy. The fifth-floor bedsit made basic provision for cooking, and there was a very small shower, but Gabriel preferred to shower with a hosepipe, several times a day, on the part of his roof terrace that faced our kitchen. Even when not showering, he was only ever scantily clad and he seized on any opportunity to promote his physique.

Using this excuse of the ants, Gabriel climbed on to the railing that separated our back balcony from his and, balancing precariously there, his toes gripping the ironwork, he peered into the guttering and into some of the larger cracks in the wall. As he wound his body this way and that, I found myself studying the dark crucifix of hair that extended from his belly to his throat, and across to both shoulders. The sooty hairs seemed to have their own movement, like iron filings responding to a magnet buried in his abdomen. Through the hair, his navel showed like a tiny, pouting mouth.

'It's no good,' Gabriel said, 'I can't see any nest,' and he jumped back down. Nevertheless he looked pleased with his exertion. He had failed to find a nest but he had made a successful display of muscles, sinews and tanned skin, and now he had an excuse to shower again.

The American newspapers I worked for were friendly and approachable, but selling articles to the British press was an ignominious business and I hated it. London was four hours ahead of us, and I had to get up early to listen to the news and see if there was anything I might be required to write about. If I did write a report it was finished and filed by mid-morning, usually to be nudged off the page later by bloodier events in Bosnia. Either way, I had the rest of the day to work on longer articles or to wander the streets of Buenos Aires. I spent much of the time wandering, in fact sometimes I walked for hours, until my mind and body were hazy with heat. Often I got lost, and once I missed a bus-stop and ended up in a depot outside the city, drinking maté and discussing free love with a bus-driver. Yet somehow it was easier to lose myself physically in the city's streets, thus presenting myself with the challenge of getting home, than to sit at my desk tackling a more abstract, emotional disorientation.

One afternoon, I strolled to a favourite library, the only one I knew where it was possible to look at the books without filling in forms. Browsing among the bookshelves, I picked out an old, thumbed copy of Eva Perón's autobiography, *La Razón de mi Vida*. Once compulsory reading in Argentine schools, then banned with an equal fervour, 'My Life's Cause' was now simply allowed to exist as the banal work of Peronist propaganda it had always been. Rejected even by its Spanish ghostwriter, who complained that his subject wanted to appear 'idealised, a myth', it was not so much an autobiography as a panegyric to General Perón, though laced with Evita's own favourite obsession: her hatred of wealth, which she saw as the root of the worker's suffering. The mere thought of this injustice, Evita wrote, 'produced a stifling feeling, as though, being unable to remedy the evils that I witnessed, I had not sufficient air to breathe . . . I think that, just as some people have a special tendency to feel beauty differently and more intensely than do people in general, and therefore become poets or painters or musicians, I have a special inherent tendency to feel injustice with unusual and painful intensity.'

This deluxe edition of 'My Life's Cause' included portrait photographs of Evita in her various roles. She posed in a gala dress by Jamandreu or visiting a sick girl in one of the many hospitals that bore her name. One picture showed her addressing the crowds from the Government House balcony in the Plaza de Mayo. Her red, shouting mouth matched fingernails which were coiled into a fist ready for fighting. 'Sometimes I've wanted to hit people in the face,' Evita had once confessed. That aggression was palpable, even in the pictures that showed her smiling. Her looks were compelling, but she was hardly the classic beauty of Peronist mythology.

A large man came into the library then, sighing loudly and muttering about the devilish heat. Since I was the only other person in the room I felt bound to acknowledge these remarks with a smile which I hoped was also a little reproving.

'But it's all right once you're inside, isn't it?' he said, sitting down at the table next to mine. The man was tall, over six foot, and he had a head shaped like a bucket and a spade beard. His sleeves were rolled over his elbows to reveal densely haired arms. There was a waxing crescent of sweat at his armpits.

I nodded at the pleasantry, smiled again and looked pointedly back at 'My Life's Cause'. But I was aware of the man's continued sideways gaze and I realised that I was not easily going to end our communication. Most likely, he had guessed that I was foreign and was curious to talk to me.

'They have good books here, haven't they – what are you reading about?'

'I'm reading about Evita,' I replied, not smiling this time and barely raising my eyes from the book.

'Our Evita, eh? And where are you from?'

'From England.'

'England. I see.' The great beard seemed to tremble a little and the man nodded in a suspicious gesture of appraisal which was now familiar to me. It meant 'I've got your number. You think you're better than us.'

I tried a smile again, meaning to convey, 'I don't think I am better: let's leave it at that.'

'Of course the weather in England is appalling,' the man said. 'Winter there must be dreadful.'

I had decided, as a rule, to agree with this sort of comment, consoling myself that it was born of resentment or envy. 'Yes, it's pretty awful,' I agreed.

'And I've heard London is very expensive.'

'Yes.'

'And dirty.'

I wondered why he should pick on me in this way when I had done nothing to provoke him. I had not, as far as I knew, committed any of the crimes of Englishness: I had not acted in a pompous or superior way. I had not disparaged his country; in fact here I was reading one of Argentina's most important historical documents.

'Yes, I suppose it is a bit dirty.'

The man was pleased to be making ground. His beard quivered with anticipation. The muscles in his arm flexed perceptibly; he was clearly moving in for the kill. I made mental preparation for the Falklands question.

'And my friend said there are so many things you can't get in England. He said you can't even get oranges.'

In a city where deliveries of fruit and vegetables were regularly delayed by bad weather and industrial disputes, this was too much.

'That's absurd,' I snapped. 'Of course you can get oranges. You can get a much wider range of produce there than you can get here and it's usually cheaper.'

The man's eyes flashed triumph. I had revealed myself to be a pompous imperialist after all. He sat back a little in his seat; his hands made as if to roll the shirt sleeves tighter, the better to fight me.

'I find that hard to believe,' he said softly. 'I bet you can't get avocados.'

'You can get avocados at half the price of the ones here!' I felt blood rush to my face. 'And you can get artichokes and parsnips and spinach and mushrooms. Tell me where you can get mushrooms in Buenos Aires?'

The man grimaced in disproportionate disgust. 'Who wants mushrooms? They grow in shit. What about aubergines? Can you get those in London?'

'Of course you can get aubergines!'

'Well, that's not what my friend said,' he paused, momentarily defeated. The man seemed to search his thoughts for ammunition, then his eyes lit up. 'You can't get *zapallito*, can you?'

There was no getting round the truth of this. 'We don't have *zapallito*, but—'

'Ha!'

'—*but* we have courgettes which taste exactly the same—'

'Ha ha!'

'—they're just a different shape.'

A *better* shape, I wanted to say. My heart was pounding with jingoistic indignation now and I could see that my adversary was flushed beneath his beard. We might have spent the rest of the afternoon at this horticultural re-enactment of the Falklands War had it not been for a mediation from the other side of a stack of shelves. The soft cough was a reminder that we were not, after all, alone in the library.

'I would really like to get on with some work, now, if you don't mind,' I said coolly.

'By all means.' The man raised his eyebrows and shrugged with Italian exaggeration, to show that I had taken a few innocent remarks in bad part. But I was too aggrieved to concentrate on the book after that, the photographs of Evita irritated me with their self-satisfaction and, anyway, my thoughts raced with kumquats, logan-berries, *radicchio* and greengages. What was the mild pleasure of *zapallito* when set against these exotica? Soon I decided to go home and gathered up my things. I nodded a frosty 'goodbye' to the bearded man and made for the exit, passing the throat-clearer who had interrupted our fight. He was a man of about twenty and he touched my arm as I passed, momentarily detaining me. He looked slightly embarrassed and, sensing that he was going to apologise for his bellicose compatriot, or make some gesture of solidarity, I bent down, moving my face close to his.

'I have a friend who went to London too,' the young man whispered. 'He said that English girls are very pretty, and I see that he was right.' He smiled and deliberately moistened his lips, as if in anticipation of a meal. I had smelt the morning's coffee turning sour on his breath before I pulled my sleeve away and marched on towards the door.

I walked home from the library in a rage, exacerbated by the difficulty of crossing the world's widest road. It was still feverishly hot and, on our avenue, the Paraguayans in their pits had taken a break from digging to concentrate on looking up skirts. Jokes in Guaraní swirled around my ankles as I stalked by. At home, I climbed out of the lift on the fifth floor, only to be greeted by Gabriel, who was loitering on the landing between our front doors, in a pair of boxer shorts. 'You look tired,' he said with unctuous concern. 'How are you feeling?' I felt a moment's apprehension of that furry chest, which seemed to invite my head to rest against it, to confide and weep.

Gabriel had a great lust to know about people's feelings. If ever I made casual reference to a bad mood, he tried to coax a more detailed agony from me. Why did I say I was frustrated, why dispirited? Was there not something more *fundamentally* wrong with me, with my relationship? Was I, at heart, *unhappy*?

'I feel fine,' I lied.

Gabriel was a psychologist. Then again, so many people in Buenos Aires were psychologists. Raquel joked that there were more psychologists in the city than human beings. With growing middle-class unemployment, it was a popular choice of profession: you needed no particular qualifications to set up a consultancy – not all 'analysts' had studied psychoanalysis – and there was an apparently unending supply of psyches in need of help.

Often described as the world capital of psychoanalysis, Buenos Aires was said to have three times as many analysts per head as New York. The head of the International Monetary Fund had recently gone so far as to criticise *porteños'* self-absorption. If they wanted the country to advance economically, he had said, they ought to spend more on the poor and less on their psyches. The remark enraged Raquel. 'How are we supposed to get over all these things that have happened to us?' she cried. 'Doesn't he want the country to recover?'

I made as if to agree with her, but secretly I sided with the IMF: the extent of the psychoanalytic culture was, indeed, remarkable. Newspapers devoted a page a day to it, bookshops were filled with volumes on self-help – innocently pronounced 'sell-hell'. Daytime television was dominated by classes on empowerment and renewal. Many were the conversations that began, 'My analyst says . . .'

It was at first funny, and later sinister, to see how the whole city lived in the grip of psychoanalysis. In the middle classes, everyone had an analyst, whom they were apt to consult on anything, from what clothes to wear to a party to career moves or health matters that would have been better put to a doctor. Argentine analysts occupied the perch that might more properly be given to fairy-godmothers. Here was a friend and wizard rolled into one, a person whose dedication to your well-being extended far beyond the walls of the consulting room. Late into the night, as she sat up in bed watching television, Raquel continued to take calls from patients worried about a range of concerns. One man kept her up to date on the functionings of his bowels.

Many *porteños* met their analysts socially, although there was an understanding that it was not professional to do so. Others arranged to spend the summer in the same resort as their analysts or, should their schedules coincide while holidaying in Europe, sought them out in the hotels of Paris, London or Rome. When it was really not possible to break the long summer vacation with a few vital sessions on the couch, clients expected to keep in touch by telephone and fax (the man with the bowel problem had once pursued Raquel across Europe with faxes). In the event of an emergency, holidaying analysts had to find time to offer telephonic succour to the patient back in Buenos Aires. An emergency, as far as I could see, might be a fit of tears after a marital row, or a job interview that had gone badly.

It struck me that there was something vain and lazy about this ubiquitous need to be probed and helped. I was reminded of the woman in the café I had heard on my first evening, and her casual comment, 'Frankly I'm traumatised.' Trauma was an easy commodity in Buenos Aires. The accent, the sing-song cadence that was peculiar to Argentine Spanish, lent itself irresistibly to melodrama: one would *want* to have traumas with such a language in which to express them.

Therapy seemed a logical response to the events that had tormented Argentina in the 1970s, but actually it had been popular for decades before that. The city's close cultural links to Europe and the huge Jewish population – outside Israel, the community was second in size only to New York's – ensured the early arrival of Freud's invention. It was a mark of intellectual distinction to seek analysis in the 1940s and the leisured wealthy went three times a week. 'Psychoanalysis came here on the arm of culture, not medicine,' Andrés Rascovsky, descended from a prestigious line of psychoanalysts, told me. 'That helped its evolution into a way of expressing intellectual opposition to the social, moral and religious repression perpetrated by the state.'

During the 1970s, the analyst's role changed dramatically. Psychoanalysis was now no longer a tool with which to examine the individual subconscious but a channel for the tacit registering of non-conformity with the state. Young men and women, some of them guerillas, attended group analysis in order to express and exchange ideas that could be mooted neither at home nor in public, because the military had declared them 'subversive'.

Just as priests took up politics in Guatemala and El Salvador, many psychoanalysts abandoned their professional neutrality and declared themselves against the regime. By connecting like-minded patients with one another, and providing a forum for discussion, they played a vital role in marshalling intellectual opposition to the dictatorship. Not surprisingly, then, they topped the list of subversives, and hundreds of analysts and their patients disappeared. One woman I met was haunted by the knowledge that she had saved her life by missing a group analysis session in 1977; that afternoon all the other members of the group had disappeared.

Now that they had nothing to fear from free expression, why did *porteños* still flock to psychoanalysis? I asked everyone I knew – and everyone I knew was in analysis – and the answer was disconcerting: people believed that a period of psychoanalysis was actually essential to the forming of a healthy personality. 'I would be worried', one woman told me, 'if my daughter brought home a boyfriend who had never had analysis. I think it would indicate a dangerous lack of introspection.'

A brave few admitted that they had psychoanalysis to be fashion-able and, from what Raquel told me, that was not an unusual reason. She had once refused to treat a woman who was 'traumatised' because her husband had given her a blue car, when she had asked him for a red one. 'For too many people an analyst is another status symbol,' she said. 'They get the smart car, the expensive house, the mink coat – and then they get the best psychoanalyst money can buy.'

The school of therapy most popular among *porteños* was that of Jacques Lacan, a French disciple of Freud. As far as I could make out from a book Raquel had lent me, Lacan had odd, possibly sadistic ideas about human relations. He tested clients' resolve by making them wait hours and, on occasion, days to see him. He also believed that a session could be broken off following a key revelation on the part of the patient – in which case the full hour would still be payable. One analyst I met boasted privately that he could 'do' six patients in an hour, charging each the full rate.

'Lacanian theory gives the analyst the most incredible licence to exploit his patient. You can end up paying a hundred dollars for a session that only lasts fifteen minutes,' said my friend Martín. 'The psychoanalysis industry in this city moves millions of untaxed dollars, because analysts always ask to be paid in cash and they don't give receipts.'

The young editor of a fashion magazine, Martín was our link to the jet set, or the *farándula*, as it was called in Argentina. Once or twice a month he invited us to parties which were to launch a new perfume or body lotion. Since I went for the free wine and canapés, perhaps I deserved the feelings of humiliation they inevitably induced in me. The parties were crowded with young models, minimally dressed, laughing and dancing in a hard, exaggerated way that was affected for the photographers. Teenage girls, absurdly dressed up as the product being launched, circulated among the guests perfuming them or dispensing sachets of body lotion as required.

For all his scepticism about psychoanalysis, Martín had it himself, and he was prone to make all the fashionable remarks about it, confessing that he was a 'therapy junkie' and wondering how he would cope when his analyst went on holiday. In Buenos Aires it was very stylish to be enslaved to your therapist. Yet Martín confessed that he often found it difficult to follow his analyst's reasoning. 'Sometimes I haven't the faintest idea what she's on about. But analysis is all anybody talks about at the shows so I keep having it. I think many people have analysis because it's a way of showing that you are wealthy, glamorous and clever.'

The point, of course, was that you might be none of these things, but keeping up the analyst was a way of keeping up appearances. In times of hardship, it was often the very last economy to be made.

It was commonly said that psychoanalysis had replaced the confessional in Buenos Aires. I felt rather that it was a national hobby, a game in which one was naughty and got ticked off – a forgivable indulgence, perhaps, and, as addictions go, not too dangerous. What seemed less forgivable was that children should be made to play the same game. Many *porteños* were initiated into the cycle of trauma-and-therapy as infants, when the stuff of their psyches would surely not bear much scrutiny. I met a couple who were sending their two-year-old to an analyst 'because she has problems showing affection to the new baby'. A male friend had been sent to an analyst, twenty years previously, over difficulties to do with toilet training and had never spent much time out of therapy since. State schools all had trained therapists on site to deal with children with specific problems, but in the private schools, attended by nearly two-thirds of children in Buenos Aires, the resident psychologists' role was powerful indeed. His job was to 'evaluate' the intelligence of incoming pupils, then to 'monitor' their performance.

'How could that be bad? It's a very good thing indeed!' cried Marilín, a public relations consultant who had offered to introduce me to 'celebrities'. 'It works wonders for teenagers, you know.'

Marilín expounded the virtues of child-analysis to me one afternoon as we sat on the terrace of La Biela, the most fashionable café in Buenos Aires in the elegant Recoleta neighbourhood and a cogent symbol of the establishment. During the Dirty War, La Biela was bombed regularly, but the staff and clientele weathered the crises with aplomb. *Cafecitos* and croissants were served as usual between bombs.

Marilín told me that her daughter had been evaluated at 70 per cent when she started her primary education, but later her grades had slipped to 60 per cent. 'She had to see the psychologist for two years,' Marilín explained. 'He made her understand, at a sub-conscious level, that she wasn't a baby any more and that she had to make more of an effort. After that her grades improved. It was a very good thing for her.' She tapped a perfectly manicured fingernail emphatically on the table top.

Stretched out in front of us, a sea of extravagantly coiffed and tinted heads were bent in the afternoon ritual of coffee-drinking and soul-baring. I could not help marvelling at these women, at the amount of time and money that must be invested in such immaculate looks. The beauty of *porteño* women was legendary. Charles Darwin, passing through Buenos Aires in 1833, wished British women had more of their 'angelic' grace. The waiters at La Biela, dark-skinned immigrants, white napkins folded over their arms, stood and watched these rare creatures as if they were not quite real. Indeed many of them were *not* quite real: plastic surgery and silicon implants were *de rigueur* among the wealthy in Argentina.

Marilín, all mascara and lipstick and stick-thin, offered me the little chocolate that had come with her coffee. It was a psychological gambit. She had watched me devour my own chocolate; if I ate hers too then that would be a bonus for her: I would be fatter and she would be thinner. I was too proud to give her the satisfaction.

'Psychoanalysts can do harm as well as good,' I suggested, waving away the chocolate.

Marilín tossed her head back with a little huff of exasperation. 'Of course they can! Psychoanalysts are like dentists or hairdressers – there are millions of them, both good and bad. If you get a haircut that you don't like you don't go back to the same hairdresser, do you? The same is true of an analyst.'

'But you might not realise he was bad until it was too late, and then the damage is done! A psyche isn't the same as a hairstyle, it doesn't grow out, ready to be shaped again by someone else...'

Marilín tutted impatiently. 'Look' – she pressed conciliatory fingers on my arm – 'I'm not saying there's anything wrong with not getting analysed. I have one or two friends who aren't in analysis myself and I don't think they're weird or anything.' She glanced around the other tables and lowered her voice. 'I expect they probably just can't afford it at the moment.'

By the time they left school, many, perhaps the majority of *porteños* had experienced some probing of their psyche, and the evaluation did not stop there. A job application, even to be a shop assistant, would likely entail assessment by the company psychologist, including questions about family relationships, childhood traumas and 'aggression management'. Psychologists were at work in most large companies and many small ones, monitoring the workers' morale and efficiency. For instance, Buenos Aires' notoriously dangerous bus-drivers had been evaluated and the conclusion was that 65 per cent of them were traumatised enough to need a course of psychotherapy.

Teachers and chief executives were expected to have constant analysis, too. 'That's only right and proper,' a father told me. 'If someone has responsibility for other people you have to make sure that he won't harm them.'

But what harm was fearful enough to merit such a sustained level of psychological 'evaluation' or 'monitoring'? In Buenos Aires there seemed to be a feeling that people's personalities were, inherently, damaging. Everyone needed fine-tuning. Marilín had insisted that it was 'arrogant' not to have therapy. 'No one is so perfect they can't be improved.'

Gabriel's job was to hang around a small factory 'assessing morale' and counselling any worker who had worries, professional or personal. From what he told me, on the occasions when we met outside the lift, the workers were frustratingly free of worries, and he was bored at work. I thought it would drive me round the bend trying to work with someone like Gabriel breathing down my neck, waiting for my psyche to make distress calls. It was bad enough living next door to him.

Yet most *porteños* were attuned to the idea of analysis and articulate on the subject of their worries. In fact, Horacio Etchegoyen, who was the president of the International Psychoanalytic Society, told me that Argentines were 'uniquely aware of psychological theory'. That was probably true. Café conversations buzzed with all the right complexes and terminology; every bedside table bore its load of 'sell-hell'.

My friends were in their late twenties and, without exception, badly off. Yet all of them were either currently receiving therapy or had received it in the past. If they had ended their treatment it was usually because they could not afford it. They had grown up on analysis and I came to realise that for most of them it represented not so much an injection of help as a permanent support system. 'If you live in a city where everything is difficult then you need someone to be on your side,' one friend said.

Yet some of them had started therapy for reasons which even they recognised as faintly absurd. Susana, a translator, went because she and her boyfriend could not agree about how to decorate their flat, and she thought this pointed up 'fundamental problems in the relationship'. Like many young people, when she could not afford to pay her analyst she did menial work for him, typing and photocopying or standing in queues at the bank. Perhaps she would have been willing to do more: she adored her analyst and often met up with him 'just because I need a hug'. Susana knew that her admiration for her mentor was risky, but when her boyfriend asked her to choose between him and the analyst, she had no compunction in choosing the analyst.

Cecilia, a thirty-year-old student of cinematography, was seeking to remedy a happy childhood. One Sunday a group of us went to have an *asado* at her home in a predominantly working-class suburb. Afterwards I commented to Cecilia that her family seemed unusually happy, the parents and three children were friendly and affectionate with one another. 'My home life is very secure and totally lacking in conflict,' she agreed, 'but that's not good. It's made it very difficult for me to make my own way in life. I have friends who've had a really terrible adolescence, and they've grown up much faster.'

Cecilia had spent ten years working at a variety of jobs to support her studies, and her analysis addiction. During *la híper*, the years of hyperinflation, she had ended up paying 80 per cent of her waitressing wage to her psychoanalyst, which meant, ironically, that she had to move back home and live with the very parents whose kindness she was trying to escape. 'My father's a car mechanic and he thought I was mad,' she told me. 'If I ever asked him for any money he said, "If you've got it to spend on therapy you don't need any more." He had a point.'

Cecilia was slight and pretty, with an appealing gap between her front teeth, and she always seemed to be happy; at least she laughed easily. But even when she was laughing she would insist, in her sing-song *porteño* accent, that really she was traumatised.

'In Buenos Aires we have two addictions: coffee and psychoanalysis. Times have to be hard – I mean *really* hard – before people give those up,' said Alicia, so painfully thin that she risked being engulfed by her sofa, if not by her melancholy. We were sitting in her apartment near the botanical gardens on a mercifully pleasant day when the humidity was not too high and the pressure not too low. The squat women from the Red Cross who usually sat on street corners, selling blood-pressure readings and recommending extra salt in the diet, had disappeared into the parks and shops. We would be safe, for the afternoon at least, from the tyranny of the weather.

Alicia poured thick black coffee into tiny cups and offered me a little pink sachet of artificial sweetener. 'Argentina is a mysterious place,' she said, and she looked for a moment really weighed down by the mystery. 'There's the sense of melancholy – which is what tango is all about – and there's a strong culture of machismo. It's a very unequal society compared to Britain or France. In other countries you go to a psychoanalyst because you are ill, but that isn't the case here. In Buenos Aires it's completely usual to have psycho-analysis, because people's opportunities are so few and there's so much frustration. In a sense *everyone* here is ill.'

A popular radio programme, made by the patients of a psychiatric hospital, traded on this paradox. In a society where everyone is unbalanced, its slogan went, only the mad are really sane.

Alicia was twice divorced. She called herself a history lecturer, but what they paid her at the university came nowhere near a living wage, so she worked long hours in a boutique to make ends meet. In some respects she was typical of her once-moneyed class: she cultivated the appearance of wealth – the flat, though tiny, was cleaned every day by a uniformed maid. In fact Alicia had little money to spare, and she spent most of it on therapy. This was in spite of the fact that she had serious reservations about psychoanalysis. She blamed the break-up of her marriage on an analyst, and she was convinced that many of them were taking money from people who did not need treatment. 'They let people who have perfectly normal worries embark on treatments that are going to take six or seven years and cost a fortune. Some analysts refuse to see you unless you promise to go three times a week. It's a wonder anyone can afford that.'

Yet most of Alicia's friends found ways to afford therapy. 'I know people whose salaries are so meagre they don't know how they're going to get to the end of the month,' she said, 'but they still have psychoanalysis. It's the only way to survive here.'

That same premise, that it was actually impossible to live in Buenos Aires unless you had a psychoanalyst, was put to me with fascinating regularity. Nor was it simply an argument of the introspective wealthy – the experience of my badly paid friends showed that. One had described psychoanalysis as 'a way of opening a breathing space in the midst of the chaos'. *Buenos Aires te mata* – the city would kill you unless you were psychologically equipped to defend yourself against it.

But how could it be that a whole community needed therapy simply to *survive*? Where were the forces of oppression, now that Argentina was no longer a dictatorship? Was there evidence that the treatment was working? How would the *porteños* know when they were cured? I hinted at self-indulgence and Alicia's eyes filled with tears. 'You don't understand what it's like,' she said. 'We're stranded here at the end of the world. We don't know who we are or where we belong. We've been forgotten by everyone.'

After leaving Alicia's I sat in the park and watched children playing on a dusty patch of ground meanly supplied with a swing, a slide and a climbing frame. Most of the children were accompanied by domestic servants, girls from Bolivia and Paraguay, who sat on benches chattering with the relief of compatriots. 'This city has been deformed by its obsession with psychoanalysis,' Alicia had said, as she showed me to the door. 'I've mortgaged my life for the sake of therapy.' I was touched by her melancholy and thinness. Suddenly I found tears coming to my eyes, but I did not know if they were for Alicia or because of the poignancy of the dusty playing ground.

The principal streets of Buenos Aires started at the port and radiated outwards for many miles, until finally, exhausted of buildings, they dissolved into the pampa. To imagine the magnitude of the pampa was to get a sense of the immensity of the space that oppressed Buenos Aires. One of the world's largest cities lived surrounded by nothing.

The first architects of the city were entranced by the pampa. Here was a city, on the west bank of the River Plata's estuary, that could grow for ever. But they never thought about its isolation. How would Buenos Aires fare with only the sea and the pampa for company? How would it communicate with the rest of the country, those cities thousands of miles inland? In 1983, the president had proposed moving the capital to a city in the centre of Argentina, but the concept was unworkable. Argentines, more than a third of whom lived in Greater Buenos Aires, could not contemplate the idea of moving deeper into the awesome landscape of their vast country. The interior symbolised an unknown violence. In 1845, Domingo Sarmiento, a philosopher, and later president, evoked a terrifying image of this unpopulated territory as inherently evil; he felt that its magnitude stamped upon the Argentine character 'a certain stoical resignation to death by violence, which is regarded as one of the inevitable probabilities of existence'.

When *porteños* talked about their addiction to psychoanalysis – and they were often as fascinated by it as I was – it was curious how often they echoed Alicia's tearful entreaty. Buenos Aires was a city stuck 'at the end of the world'. It sounded like a romantic assignation, and yet it was a genuine source of pain. Faced with the pampa's infinite horizon, where could the citizens look but back across the ocean to the continent their ancestors had left? Ninety-seven per cent of Argentines were descended from Europeans and many of them, especially the snobs, felt themselves to be the victims of a dreadful accident of history. They had been stranded; they ought, by rights, to be in London, Paris or New York. Their solution to this dilemma was to demand the best of both worlds. Furniture, fine foods, clothes, ideas were all bought in. 'Our entire country is imported,' wrote Borges. 'Everyone here is really from somewhere else.'

One of the most fashionable psychoanalysts in Buenos Aires lived in a leafy side-street off one of those avenues that were heading for the pampa. Suave, handsome, a fluent English-speaker, Eduardo spent several weeks a year as a visiting lecturer at Columbia University. His apartment seemed to hark after the style of a New York loft: it was minimally furnished and dominated by black and white. Perhaps these contrasts were necessary to a man whose business was to deal in shades of grey.

'My brain is the only instrument I have,' said Eduardo as we drank fizzy water in his consulting room, and it looked, from the expanse of his forehead, as if it might be a big brain. 'People come to see me because they cannot do something. They cannot pass exams or give blood tests or they cannot achieve an orgasm. They feel that I can help them to do or accomplish something.'

There was modern art on the wall and the muffled sound of a child lurching about upstairs. I found that the competing blacks and whites of the consulting room played tricks on my eyes; the fizzy water pricked my nostrils.

'In Argentina it's particularly difficult because people are not trained to accomplish at school,' said Eduardo. 'The training you receive is how to get through school fast, copying and cheating in exams, so that all your wit is directed towards deception. The main achievement is *viveza criolla*, to be able to skip over your obligations. Kids have to pay reverence to the flag and sing the national anthem, learn about nineteenth-century generals, but most of the people I get do not know the ABC of thinking – they're naive, they put the cart before the horse. They don't see the basic things, so you have to teach them. Sometimes that means saying "Try wearing this tie, that suit."'

It was hot even with the fan on, and Eduardo's shirt was partly unbuttoned to reveal a deeply tanned chest, as smooth as Gabriel's was hairy. He was a smooth talker, too, and I was fighting to concentrate and not let my mind slip against the patina of his words. One would need to be glamorous to be analysed by such an attractive man, I thought, but I could understand the temptation to confide one's secrets to that smooth brown chest. I wondered vaguely if he had ever made love to one of his patients on the couch.

Then, with barely a change in cadence, Eduardo said something quite different. 'Look what happened here. A few people protested against the government and they responded by torturing and murdering thirty thousand. Don't you think there must be something *wrong* in the essence of a human being for that to happen?'

Was that the reason why so many people had analysis? Were Argentines, subconsciously, trying to correct the design flaw that had ruined their history? Marilín had almost said as much. 'We Argentines are different,' she had told me, that sunny afternoon at La Biela. 'Don't you think there might be something wrong with us?'

One evening Raquel invited me to try out her new couch, a present from an ex-patient, in lieu of many unpaid sessions.

I perched tentatively on the fashionably zig-zagged structure. I had just been helping Santiago to do his English homework and was astonished to find that, in an exercise titled 'What does your mother/father do?', 'psychoanalyst' was one of the eight possible answers, along with doctor, lawyer and housewife. Santiago had learned how to spell the word in English, but he could not pronounce it in either language. We had discussed the possibility of his getting away with 'doctor' in the oral exam.

'Assuming you could put Argentina on the couch,' I asked Raquel, 'what would you find?'

'A country that has no identity, that doesn't know what it wants to be. People who can't trust one another.' She thought for a moment, swinging in her analyst's chair. 'I think part of the reason so many *porteños* have analysis is that they feel lost. During the dictatorship, they were told, "you can't do this, you can't go there". Subconsciously people miss the voice of authority and they're looking for a substitute. They want their analyst to replace the voice of the dictator.'

I lay back on the couch and found my feet were raised disconcertingly higher than my head; presumably this was to aid the thought processes necessary for a meaningful exchange with the analyst. The shelves on the wall above me supported some professional paraphernalia: a few primitivist sculptures from Peru; the complete works of Freud and of Lacan. There were cards with sentimental poems of gratitude printed on them, possibly from patients who felt better now. I closed my eyes and tried to imagine what it would be like to be frightened, really frightened, of torture or death, or, conversely, to be frightened of democracy. I found that I could not imagine such a fear, the privileges of my background and upbringing made it impossible. But what I did know now impressed itself upon me like a talisman. I felt I knew what it was like to be forgotten. I knew what it was like to live at the end of the world.

CHAPTER FOUR

The Wall of Silence

THERE WAS A word I kept hearing: *bronca*. An Italo-Spanish fusion, like most Argentines themselves, the word implied a fury so dangerously contained as to end in ulcers. People felt *bronca* when they waited for an hour to be served at a bank, and then the service was bad because the cashiers all had *bronca* too. *Bronca* crackled down the crossed telephone lines and stalked the checkout queues in supermarkets with hopeful names like Hawaii and Disco.

I could easily lose an hour in one of these queues on a Friday evening, among women who looked like refugees nudging towards a border, their trolleys piled high with items that might have been grabbed in an evacuation. Coca-Cola and meat, big bleeding hunks of it, were essentials in Buenos Aires, and weekends were provided for as if they were sieges. Blood from the meat dripped on to the floor and the checkout counter and the cashiers, moody under their baseball caps, kept cloths beneath the counter to wipe the blood away.

Despite the forced cheer of the pop music and baseball caps, going to the supermarket in Buenos Aires was a humiliating experience. It began with a scuffle for trolleys and usually ended with an argument about small change: since there was a severe shortage of coins in Argentina, most prices had to be negotiated. There was a queue to deposit personal items, which could not be taken beyond the security guards, and, once inside, there were queues for meat, for vegetables, for bread, and then the worst queue of all, to get out. Some people simply could not stand the ordeal, and every so often shoppers disappeared, abandoning their fully loaded trolleys in different corners of the supermarket. Tears got the better of some, and once I witnessed a marriage break down in the fresh-produce section. 'I've found out about your lover,' a woman calmly told her husband as she dropped tomatoes into the bag he held open. 'Let's have done with this charade.'

As they waited for their turn at the till, people tended to smoke or eat, sampling the produce that was conveniently close to hand. The shelves lining routes to the checkout were dotted with half-finished packets of crisps and biscuits, or even open jars of imported jam, tasted briefly and discarded. A dreadful tension hung over the queuers and tempers flared easily. 'Why is this country such a shit-hole?' strangers asked one another. 'How did we get like this?'

Everyone had *bronca*. The weather, with its cruel regime of heat and thunderstorms, had *bronca*. The lift had *bronca*, groaning as it carried us between floors. Máximo's *bronca* was so pernicious that he could contain it only with music. Maradona, the newspapers reported, had recently relieved his *bronca* by firing an airgun at the journalists camped outside his house, injuring one.

I had *bronca*, too. Sometimes I stood in the kitchen, watching the ants and listening to the neighbours shout at one another, or I gazed impotently at the fizzy evolution of creatures in our bathroom's open drain – whatever they were, they resisted every sort of extermination. Scott Joplin called five times in a morning to torment me with 'The Entertainer', or Bosnia pushed me off the foreign pages again. On those occasions I considered my life in Argentina and felt a desperation pressing my throat.

One afternoon of particularly discomfiting heat, Raquel's *bronca* reached explosion point. Several of us were talking in her sitting room when she burst in like a cartoon housewife, wearing an apron over her night-dress and brandishing a smoking frying pan. The smell of burned onions drifted dismally in behind her. 'I'm fifty-one. Soon I'll die and I won't have done *anything* with my life,' she shrieked. Then she turned on her heel and rushed back to the kitchen, where we heard her making a passionate clatter of things. Santiago's father, Pablo, raised his eyebrows, because he knew that the recrimination was for him.

If Raquel was exasperated by her third husband, the other two, by her own account, had been much worse. The first was unfaithful. The second, she confided quite casually, had threatened to have her 'disappeared' during the dictatorship. Then, when Raquel's uncle stepped in with a handsome bribe, the police gratefully turned the tables, offering to do away with her recalcitrant husband instead. 'Say the word and we can put him at the bottom of the river,' they assured her. She had declined and now she even seemed to get on well with her second ex – but I wondered how many other husbands and wives in Buenos Aires had consigned one another to watery graves.

I had not known whether to laugh at Raquel's extraordinary story when she told it, or to be horrified by it. There were a number of euphemisms for the excesses of the last dictatorship: it was the Process, the Repression or the Terror. Many people described it with a phrase invented by the dictators themselves, *la guerra sucia*, the 'Dirty War'. Whatever they called it, everyone in Buenos Aires had a story about relations who had been tortured or neighbours who had disappeared. I wanted to hear the stories, and yet, when I did hear them, my instinct was to disbelieve them. What had happened in the 1970s seemed too terrible for truth and logic, and the more I heard, the less I understood. My brain wanted to comprehend and classify the information, and could not.

People rarely talked about the Dirty War, except in fitful anecdotes which were like fragments of memory salvaged from a wreckage too deeply buried for proper exploration. Sometimes they frowned as they told of their experiences, shrugging and shaking their heads, as if their own ears spontaneously rejected the evidence of their mouths. When the revelations came, they were atrocious, nightmarish, and sometimes, like Raquel's, they were blackly funny. There was the one about a man who had been abducted and tortured then, months later, invited out to dinner by his oppressor, to show that there were 'no hard feelings'. A girl was taken to the opera by her torturer. There were macabre tales of muddled bureaucracy leading to the wrong people getting 'disappeared'. Thanks to crossed lines, death threats went to the wrong homes. When the inevitable call arrived at the home of the writer Jorge Luis Borges, a prominent anti-Peronist, his mother gave the would-be assassin their address and told him to hurry, as she was ninety-five years old and had been waiting to die for years.

'Sometimes you have to laugh about what happened, or you'd lose your mind,' said Patricia Bernardi, a member of the Argentine Forensic Anthropological Team. These eight men and women in their early thirties had been trained by Americans to find mass graves and identify victims of state terror, a job no established Argentine forensic had wanted to learn. The team not only worked in Argentina, but travelled all over a continent which had proved itself inefficient at most things but not murder. In the course of their grisly work they had evolved a particularly black sense of humour. The walls of their small office, eight blocks from the Congress, were decorated with pictures of dancing Mexican skeletons and a giant poster from the Chamber of Horrors at Madame Tussaud's. 'The people who disappeared were our generation, our friends, and we've made a political commitment to finding them,' Patricia said. 'We have to make sure this never happens again.'

On Thursday afternoons I sometimes left the house, walked down our avenue, past the libidinous murmurings of the Paraguayans, across the world's widest road and down to the Calle Florida, a busy, pedestrianised street full of bars, ice-cream parlours and electronics shops. This was modern Buenos Aires: Calle Florida throbbed day and night with American pop music, the foreign rhythms punctured now and then by simulated warfare from the games arcades. Shop windows were full of the latest permutations of denim imposed by fashion houses thousands of miles away. Close by, there was a cinema that specialised in arty European films and another that showed a continuous programme of hard-core sex. Its publicity shots were of blonde women glancing backwards at the camera over buttocks that were so pink and shiny they seemed to cry out for the addition of a curly tail. One of the most potent myths about the Argentine *macho* was that he favoured sodomy.

To run the gauntlet of this brash and noisy street was a strange prelude to the Plaza de Mayo, which opened up a few yards from Calle Florida's end. The capital's most important square still retained much of its colonial architecture. Here stood the city chambers, the cathedral and the government house, named La Casa Rosada for a pink façade that had originally been achieved by mixing pigs' blood with whitewash. The Plaza de Mayo had been the stage for the most important scenes in the nation's history. Revolutions had been born and quashed in this small square, generals had toppled presidents, then been toppled in their turn. Maradona greeted ecstatic crowds from the presidential balcony after Argentina's victory in the 1986 World Cup. All the nation's triumphs and failures had been marked here with cheers and celebrations, or riots, gunfire and the spattered blood of men, women and pigs.

It was in the Plaza de Mayo that more than a million workers from all over the country gathered to demand the freedom of the Minister of Labour, Juan Perón, imprisoned in October 1945 by a president who was fearful of his charisma and his powerful appeal to the working classes. That historic day, the *porteño* wealthy had looked out of their windows and seen the streets streaming with people, a provincial 'infestation'. There had not been enough room in the square for all the *descamisados*, the 'shirtless' workers for whom Perón was a hero. Old black-and-white footage showed crowds banked up all the way down the main avenues that led into the square. They hung from the trees and lamp-posts, they demanded Perón for their leader, and they got him – four months later he was president.

Argentina had changed for good that afternoon: never again would power and privilege be the natural allies they had been since colonialisation. A new phenomenon was born then that would hypnotise the nation, and ultimately tear it apart. It would come to be judged so dangerous that all the words associated with it – 'Perón', 'Peronism', 'Evita' – would later be banned in Argentina for nearly twenty years.

After Perón's triumphant election in 1946, it became traditional for people to flock to the Plaza de Mayo on national holidays. They came to see Perón, and later they came to see his wife, for in 1948 Evita started to make speeches alongside her husband. It was from the small square balcony at the front of the Casa Rosada that she harangued the crowd with a heady mix of love and violence. When she died, millions mourned here. Then in 1955 the square filled with corpses when a crowd that had gathered to celebrate Nation Day was bombed, anticipating the coup that was to topple Perón.

'I must have seen every major gathering from 1970 onwards,' said Pablo, whose office overlooked the Plaza de Mayo. 'I saw Perón's last speech. I saw Galtieri announce that the Malvinas had been invaded in April 1982 – that was a tremendous day. Then I was here when the war was lost and a mob tried to storm the Casa Rosada. We were trapped in the office until midnight because of the tear-gas.'

And it was in this same square that the Mothers of May Square gathered every Thursday afternoon, as they had done since 1977, to proclaim the greatest injustice in Argentine history: the 'disappearance' of their children during the Dirty War. For two hours the women linked arms and walked with their ghosts, round and round the square's main monument, under the watchful eye of the president's guards.

With their handbags, their support stockings, these placid demonstrators could look simply like old ladies out for a stroll. The difference was that each wore a white scarf, embroidered with the words 'let the disappeared reappear, alive'. After so many years, they knew that this was tantamount to demanding a miracle; even so there was something moving about the women's appropriation, in cross-stitch, of such violent words. Some of them carried photographs of their children, like the ones I was used to seeing in the daily newspaper, except that here they were vastly enlarged – and there was a sinister element to the enlargement. The point of the vigil was to reclaim these men and women as individuals, not 'guerillas' or 'subversives,' and yet a fuzzy imprecision took away the individuality of each face and seemed to make it another mask of pain and injustice. The faces in the photographs were no longer personal, as they would have been on mantelpiece snapshots or tucked into wallets, but rather totems, each with a slogan. 'Disappeared, Tortured, Assassinated. Where is she now?'

I met the relations of some of these murdered youths, and heard the shameful, tragic stories of others. One mother told me how she lived in fear of sitting next to her daughter's murderer in the cinema. I heard how a teenage protester had been denounced to the police by his own parents, in the hope that his behaviour, and his homework, would benefit from a night in prison. But the police killed him. 'In effect, the parents murdered their own son,' his childhood friend, now an economist, told me. He smiled the sad, wry smile of the Argentines. 'How do you get over something like that?'

The answer, perhaps for the majority of Argentines, was that you got over it by pretending it had never happened. There was no plan to establish a museum of the Dirty War in Buenos Aires, no educational trust to explain what had happened to forthcoming generations. The most notorious torture centre, the Naval Mechanics School, where some 5,000 people died, was still used by the Navy.

Many were troubled by this vacuum and, just as there was a vocabulary to talk about the dictatorship, there was one for its aftermath. People complained of a culture of 'impunity' that let wrongdoers go unpunished, the 'wall of silence' that kept Argentina from its past. 'Memory' was debated obsessively on television and in newspaper columns, the territory disputed between those who insisted that the horrors of the past must be confronted and those who felt that the country would be healed faster if it forgot them and looked to the future.

To remember or to forget – which was the right course for Argentina now? The events of the *proceso* were only fifteen years old, yet they were distancing themselves in time, drawing the cloak of history over themselves, and there was a fear that, if they were not scrutinised now, they might one day re-emerge to do untold psychological damage. 'Although people feel a need to forget the past, it doesn't help in the long run,' said Lita Stantic, a film director who had made a film called *A Wall of Silence*. 'Buried traumas always rebound.' The night graffitists railed against such an eventuality, scrawling 'We shall never forget' across walls and monuments.

'Everyone knows what happened in Argentina,' said Uki Goñi, a journalist who had worked closely with the Mothers during the Dirty War. 'The concentration camps are still standing, ex-torturers haven't even moved house, yet everything is secret. You never really know what's going on. There are 1,200 ex-repressors living free here. Argentina is the biggest gaol in the world, and we're stuck in it with them.'

The Mothers' weekly demonstration was a focal point for the discussion of these issues, a place to speak about the unspeakable. There were stalls with books about the disappeared in various languages. People gathered under the shade of the trees to talk about what had happened, and what it might mean for the future.

Once I watched a woman approach one of the Mothers' supporters and ask with great anxiety: 'Do you think it's possible that any of the repressors will go to heaven?'

Gently considerate of her question, the man hesitated before he answered: 'I don't think so, because they'd have to be sorry for what they did, and they aren't.'

'That's all I wanted to know,' said the woman, turning to leave. 'I just couldn't stand to think they'd got away with it.'

Helping a friend, Alejandro, clean up after supper at his house, I ventured to ask about the guerillas. Had he been tempted to join them?

'I managed to keep out of it, though many of my friends became Montoneros,' he said, 'and it was really hard to avoid it at university. It was almost as if there was no choice, you were either a guerilla, or you were an accomplice of the government. There was one friend in particular—' Alejandro paused, apparently ambushed by a memory he had long ago secured in some unvisited recess of the mind; he withdrew his arms from the washing bowl and stared into the soapy water, as if the troubling image had surfaced there, among the plates and cutlery. 'It's been such a long time since I thought of him,' he murmured.

'Who was he?'

'He was very intelligent, he was from a good background, well-off parents, his father was a conservative politician.'

'The classic Montonero background...'

'We were very close friends, but then the guy fell blindly in thrall to Perón. I remember trying to question him on some aspect of Peronism and all he would say was "If Perón said it, then it's true," as if Perón were godlike, infallible. I couldn't believe he could be so stupid. I said, "So what are you now, a prophet, for Perón?"'

There was a pained edge to Alejandro's voice and I guessed that he was reviving a frustration that had been suppressed for twenty years. He lowered his voice, mindful of the child who was playing next door: 'Of course they killed him later on.' Then he plunged his arms back into the basin, ready to forget the friend, to return this painful memory to a deeper recess in the mind.

'Why do you think so many people like that became guerillas?' I pressed on. 'What was the attraction?'

'In a way it was a generational rebellion, like the rebellions in Europe or the United States. I don't think any of us had a clear idea of what we wanted, or what the Montoneros were fighting for. We just wanted an end to the dictatorships – the country was stagnant.'

'But here the rebellion was so much more violent. So many people got killed.'

'We came from a history of violence, so when our reaction came it was bound to be violent,' said Alejandro. 'We were claustrophobic. It was illegal to read Mao Tse-tung or Marx so, of course, we all wanted to read them. It was a strange, crazy time, but sometimes I think at least there was an energy then, there was a feeling that things could change. Now people are so resigned.' He turned decisively back to the washing-up. 'It will be a very long time before we can really talk about these things.'

'What was a strange, crazy time, Daddy?' asked the child who had come padding into the room trailing a toy rabbit by one elongated ear.

There was a friendly, church-hall atmosphere at the headquarters of the Grandmothers of the Plaza de Mayo, an organisation which was searching for the living progeny of the disappeared. Women could be heard chatting and laughing in the kitchen and the kettle was always on the boil for maté. A pin-board dotted with some familiar black-and-white smiling faces might have held no drama were it not for the words underneath them: 'Do you know where they are?'

Among the thousands of young women abducted during the Dirty War, more than one hundred were known to have been pregnant. Survivors' testimony suggested that most of them had been kept alive until they gave birth, then murdered, their own lives ended in their children's beginning. The babies, born in concentration camps, were sometimes handed over to orphanages and adoption agencies. One girl was found on an orphanage doorstep with a board hung round her neck: 'I am the daughter of subversives; my parents were murdered today.'

However, most of the infants were thought to have been appropriated by police officers and army officials and sometimes by the very men who had murdered their mothers. Survivors of the Navy

Mechanics School, the most terrible concentration camp of all, reported seeing lists attached to the wall on which military staff made a note of the characteristics they were looking for in an adoptive baby. Sex, hair and eye colour were noted. On the maternity ward, officers walked among the beds, sizing up the expectant mothers. Perhaps some of the men felt ashamed of what they were doing, but for others there was evidently a perverse logic in their gruesome appropriation of these babies born of 'subversives'. In raising the children as their own, they would, in their turn, *righteously* subvert the wishes of the murdered parents. The children would be brought up to deplore those beliefs that had made their parents wayward. They would grow up loving the oppressors of their parents. There could be no more complete victory than to usurp your enemy's child and raise it to emulate and admire you instead.

The general amnesty had exonerated those guilty of war crimes in Argentina, but the appropriation of children born to the disappeared remained an offence. So, unless the adoptive parents of a 'disappeared' child could prove that they had no knowledge of his origins, they must return him to the biological family. In 1983, the government had set up a National Bank of Genetic Data, where blood samples from relatives of disappeared children were stored. The Grandmothers of May Square were investigating 217 reported cases of missing children, including babies born in captivity and young children abducted along with their parents. Using DNA testing, fifty-four children had so far been traced and twenty-five of them restored to their biological families.

But time was running out. Most of the missing children were now in their late teens, and soon they would be adults. Besides, the grandmothers were getting old, and lately the search for Argentina's lost children had been attracting controversy. Several relocated children had become hysterical, one threatening suicide, at the prospect of being parted from their 'parents'. Quite suddenly the grandmothers found themselves cast in the role, not of saviours, but of persecutors. Although the law was on their side, the rights of the adoptive parents, some of whom were known to have been torturers and murderers, were implicitly defended.

This clutch of unhappy, dislocated children stood for fears and regrets that had long been hidden. They were the offspring of a monstrous union: tyranny with amnesty. 'It's as if the ghosts of the past have caught up with us,' observed one political analyst. 'We had been trying to live as if the violence that wounded our country never took place.'

In the case of one pair of twins, in particular, all the nation's fearful secrets and mistakes came to be symbolised. DNA tests had shown that Gonzalo and Matías were the children of young *desaparecidos*; moreover, their adoptive father, a police chief, and known to have been a torturer, was probably the man who killed their mother. Following lengthy court actions, the teenagers had been sent to live with a biological uncle whose modest means and left-wing views were in absolute opposition to all they had previously known. The relationship was agonising: the twins insisted on referring to their abductors as their 'real' parents. The uncle, tormented by their rejection of their birth-mother and her ideals, declared publicly that his nephews had been 'brainwashed by their repressors'. The situation became so unhappy that a judge finally agreed to place the boys with foster-parents, but still denied them any contact with the adoptive mother or father.

Weeping and stammering, the boys now appeared on national television to defend their right to live with the father they accepted had once been a torturer. As far as they were concerned, he had fought in a 'dirty war' in which both sides killed indiscriminately. 'It was a terrible time that destroyed lots of families,' said one of the boys, 'but Argentina has to forget these old rancours because we are the ones who are paying the price.' 'Our human rights are being violated in the name of human rights,' cried the other. 'We're tired of being afraid.'

The twins' anguish touched a nerve. To many it now seemed perverse to take children away from people who loved them in order to place them with a relative, probably an elderly grandparent, who might be hard pressed to look after them or even to love them. In a later poll, 80 per cent of respondents said that the boys should be able to live with their expropriators.

For those people struggling to keep alive the memory of what had happened in the 1970s, many of whom had suffered themselves, this was a truly shocking outcome. It was the equivalent of suggesting that the children of Holocaust victims might be raised in good faith by ex-Nazis. How could a torturer possibly be a good father? How could the dead be betrayed in this way? The poll seemed horrifically symbolic of the way Dirty War crimes were being smoothed over and gradually forgotten.

In her small office, Estela Barnes de Carlotto, president of the Grandmothers, allowed a flicker of pain to cross her face. She was used to dealing daily and in a pragmatic way with cases of anguish that would test most human hearts to breaking point. Yet the example of the twins, their rejection of a family that had already suffered so much, and the championing of their cause on national television, caused her an undisguisable hurt.

'How can people say that we're tearing apart the lives of *our own grandchildren*?' she cried. 'Their lives were torn apart when their defenceless young mothers were murdered.' She leaned emphatically across the table. 'Those women had carried them for nine months, sung to them and made plans for them.'

Behind her on the wall hung a black-and-white photograph of her daughter with the date of her disappearance and the name of the man who had riddled her body with bullets shortly after she had given birth to a boy. Her daughter was dark, but Estela was fair, good-looking, rather British-looking in fact. On the walls there were drawings made by children who had been found and returned to their families, with loving notes attached to them. A childish drawing of the Grandmothers and Mothers, wearing triangles for scarves, was dedicated to Señora Barnes de Carlotto, who had spent seventeen years looking for her own grandson and had never lost hope of finding him.

'People say that it's traumatic and harmful to break up a child's home,' she told me, 'but the psychology we use has proved that removing a child from a deceitful family and restoring his or her real identity can only ever be healing and beneficial.'

All the children so far restored to their families had found the transition traumatic; one girl described it as 'being born again'. Yet psychological, and even medical, research suggested that the pain of being uprooted was better than the insidious damage of living, unknowingly, with the 'enemy'. After a period of settling in, a recuperated child's school-work and confidence often improved dramatically. There was some evidence of children even experiencing a sudden acceleration in growth. It seemed that to live in a family where there was such an appalling secret affected a child to the extent that it could even stunt growth.

'We're not breaking up happy families, because there is no such thing as a happy family relationship based on a lie – the lie poisons everything,' Alicira Rios, the Grandmothers' legal adviser, insisted. A survivor of the concentration camps, she had helped to get a clause concerning the right to know one's identity included in the United Nations' Bill of Children's Rights. Now she had come to believe that that right was also a responsibility. 'Children have a duty to know the truth about their origins. They must know what their identity is, however painful the process.'

Estela's ambitions for her organisation were now much diminished. 'We've decided that the most important thing, taking into account the children's age, their rebelliousness and their upbringing, is the recuperation of their identity,' she said. 'We want them at least to know who they are, who their parents were and what they did. That should give them the freedom to think about what has happened, to understand it – and then to choose. But they must know the truth. The truth is always good for people.'

We have a right to know the truth, a duty to know the truth – but the truth was so hard to get a grip on in Argentina. Even the daily business of checking facts and figures with government offices and institutions threw up inconsistencies that constantly defied verification. Four official sources could not agree on the age of the president. Serious cases of corruption and murder, sometimes involving the president's family, appeared in the newspapers then promptly disappeared.

The result was a feeling of transience that afflicted much of the population, making them feel constantly insecure. What were you if the ground under your feet was always shifting, if there was no national stock of knowledge, no agreed history, no truths held to be self-evident? If nothing was certain, if nothing existed for sure, then even murders, thousands of them, could officially be denied.

Just when we thought the summer would never end, a ferocious wind swept up from the south and snuffed out the heat, putting a stop to the mini-skirts and ants. The wind was important and distinctive enough to have its own name: it was the legendary *sudestada*, the 'south-easterly' that periodically raged north from Antarctica, a bitter reminder from the world's end that there was more to Argentina than Buenos Aires. People said that the relentless, violent winds of Patagonia could drive you mad and I liked to imagine the *sudestada* accumulating insanities as it travelled cross-country, all with the purpose of letting them loose on Buenos Aires. Thus the provinces wreaked revenge on their capital for its indifference. No wonder there were so many psychoanalysts in the capital.

The wind scattered newspaper stalls, tore down trees and telephone lines. It threw the lashing rain not just downwards, but sideways, in a concerted campaign that made quick work of the flimsy umbrellas being sold on every street corner. We put out buckets and bowls to catch the water that now streamed through three holes in the roof. In bed, I pulled the blankets over my head, hoping for a night uninterrupted by water splashing on to my face. Even so, I woke in the morning with wet cheeks and strands of hair sticking to my forehead, and a momentary sensation of having wept during the night, or of having sweated off a fever.

For three days after the *sudestada* we were without electricity, which meant that there was no pump to bring us water and we had to wash at friends' houses. Various times a day we trailed up and down the 100-odd steps between our flat and the street. The prospect of going to the supermarket was too awful to contemplate, so we lived on sandwiches and steaks from the corner café.

As I was making the difficult descent one evening I met Máximo coming the other way. We were both holding candles and in the flickering light his face was crimson with dramatic patches of shadow. 'Do you know what the hell they want to do now?' – he was practically spitting with rage. 'They want to have a whole new lift put in. It's going to cost a fortune!' His free hand, gesticulating furiously, made giant tarantulas on the wall behind him.

Standing there on the spiral staircase with our guttering candles, I felt as if we were conspirators in a Shakespearian tragedy, and that I was the lily-livered boy, the one who was fearful of spilling blood. The hulk of the lift hung motionless above us in the stairwell, an eavesdropper brooding on its fate. It was nearly a hundred years old and we might be risking our lives by not having it replaced, but the cost would be astronomical. 'We have to demand a meeting about this with the administrator immediately,' Máximo hissed. 'We must keep on telephoning him until he fixes a date.' I murmured limp agreement and, as he continued upwards, and I downwards, I heard him say, 'It's all very well to come and visit Argentina, you know, but just thank God you'll leave this hell-hole one day!'

I left my extinguished candle and matches by the front door, ready for the ascent, and slipped into the evening street. In the café opposite our building the chess-players were bent motionless over their pieces, as usual; they looked as if they had not moved for weeks. Schools of black and yellow taxis swam up the road. Round the corner, the fat *asador* was plying his grill with meat, in an apron streaked with blood and grease. I walked four blocks and turned left on to the Avenida de Santa Fé, the capital's most elegant avenue.

The boutiques here were expensive and staffed by notoriously rude shop assistants. 'Don't bother looking round,' one friend of mine had been told, 'we have nothing in your size.' The cafés on Santa Fé were significantly smarter than those on our street and there was a richer texture to the voices, perfume and smoke that climbed together out of their open windows. 'He's divine – but he's my analyst!' laughed a woman in a tight suit and dark glasses. 'I'm an ecologist,' a man at another window was saying earnestly, 'and I tell you that *this city is dying*.'

Further up the road were the city's more expensive cinemas, favourite refuges of wealthy *porteños* in the summer months, because they offered superior air-conditioning. Outside each cinema, a billboard depicted garish scenes of love and violence from the current releases. The boards were copied by hand from publicity photographs and, in the hasty magnification, all the portraits were done a marginal but crucial injustice. Woody Allen's face became plumper, Sean Connery's mouth was a little too full, his neck too thick. Meryl Streep's nose was foreshortened. In each case the misrepresentation was tiny, and yet so devastating that I half wondered if it might be a case of deliberate sabotage; such clever character assassination ought not simply to be a work of coincidence. It was preferable to think that a team of anarchist billboard-painters had set out deliberately to subvert the identities of Hollywood stars, under cover of night.

I was on my way to meet Vicente, an ardent Peronist I had got to know once while waiting to interview a trade unionist about job cuts. Since the wait on that occasion had been more than an hour, Vicente and I had talked at some length. Among other pieces of information – all defiantly imparted – he had told me that he was 'proud to live in the Third World', and that he was 'proud to have been a militant in the 1970s'. Although I was clearly bourgeois, he had invited me for a coffee that day and subjected me to a history of Peronism so tedious that I may have absorbed, at best, only a tiny part of it. When, in spite of my slim contribution to the afternoon's conversation, Vicente invited me for another coffee, I suspected that he was looking for a seduction, either physical or political. I took up this second invitation all the same, because I was curious about his militancy and his defiance and I thought – if I could only concentrate this time – that I might learn something about Peronism, a phenomenon that still mystified me.

The café, when I found it, was empty but for Vicente, who was sitting in a corner reading a newspaper. Two elderly waiters were stationed at the end of the bar, glued to a television which showed images of topless women sunbathing on a Mediterranean beach. An excited voice-over marvelled at the liberated attitude of Europeans. A woman jumped out of the foaming waves, breasts bouncing. 'Let's see that again in slow-motion!' cried the voice. As the tape was rewound, the woman crouched defensively back into the sea, the smile fading from her face as she plucked her arms out of the blue sky. Frothy waves sprang away from her and raced smoothly to the horizon. Then the studio audience laughed and cheered as, once again, this Venus was made to emerge dripping from the sea.

It was embarrassing to be meeting a militant under these circumstances; I felt the nudity on screen disadvantaged me, but Vicente seemed oblivious, or at any rate used to it. He ordered me a coffee and the waiters huffed, then tossed a coin to see who would be drawn away from the television to prepare it. The one who lost still managed to execute my order without ever taking his eyes off the screen. Determined not to miss a single breast, he even contrived to walk sideways to our table, like some species of pop-eyed sea creature.

Vicente was tall and handsome in a dramatic way, with black shaggy hair that looked right for a revolutionary. As I sat down opposite him, I saw for the first time that he had a scar right across his neck. I wondered if it had anything to do with his 'militant' activities.

Vicente said, 'Today is an important day, do you know why?'

'No,' I confessed. I ought to know, but sometimes it seemed as if most of the days in the calendar had been hijacked for the honouring of battles, dignitaries and assorted occasions of national pride. The anniversary celebrated with most gusto in Buenos Aires was Gnocchi Day, playfully known as the Revolution of the 29th. On the twenty-ninth day of every month, *porteños* ate potato gnocchi. No one knew the origin of this tradition – which had evolved into a superstition – except that gnocchi were cheap, and the twenty-ninth was the last day of the financial month for many. The ritual had given rise to a popular nickname: those bureaucrats who went to work only on pay-days were fondly known as *ñoquis*.

'It's the 20th of June,' said Vicente, 'the day General Perón returned to Buenos Aires, from exile.'

'The day of the shooting at Ezeiza Airport?'

He smiled and the scar seemed to smile too. 'That's right.'

Perón's return in June 1973 had marked a watershed in the violence. Half a million people had gone to welcome *El Líder* home, all from widely different political backgrounds yet all, somehow, under the impression that Perón spoke for them and not their enemies. Everyone was for Perón, but there was no clear idea what Perón was for himself. From his exile in Madrid, the ageing general had cynically encouraged both right- and left-wing Peronists to fight on his behalf. 'Violence already reigns, and only more violence can destroy it,' he told the Montoneros, allowing them to believe that he supported Che Guevara and Castro's revolution, while the right-wingers knew he was an old-fashioned nationalist, an admirer of Mussolini. Everyone thought that Perón would answer their problems.

But their problems were just beginning. As Perón's plane was about to land, a gun battle broke out among different factions of Peronists and hundreds of people were killed or injured. Perón's plane was diverted. Later, bodies were found hanging from the trees in woodland around the airport.

'Did you go to Ezeiza?' I asked Vicente.

'No, I didn't.' He smiled with the scar again. 'But I was a member of the Peronist Youth at school. I used to go on all the demonstrations. My best friend was disappeared when he was only seventeen.'

'What were you demonstrating for? I mean, what did you want?'

Vicente looked surprised. 'We wanted Perón to come back. We

wanted a people's revolution to overthrow the dictatorship. A new social order and a new country.'

The leader of the Montoneros had spoken grandly of creating 'a totally new mankind'.

'And the canonisation of Evita?'

'Some people wanted that. I was never very religious.'

'But Perón betrayed you in the end, didn't he? When he came back he supported the right-wing Peronists, not the left-wing. Then the fighting got worse.'

'There were reactionaries within the party, the Peronist old guard. It was always going to be difficult to combat them.'

Vicente's smiling self-assurance and the naked women I could still see disporting on the television combined to make me suddenly angry. 'It seems to me that your main achievement was to bring down violence on thousands of people who had nothing to do with politics, who were innocent. You ended up tearing the country apart, all in the name of Perón, who was a megalomaniac, and Evita, who stood for nothing, if not hatred.'

Vicente took a sip of coffee and gave me a measured look. 'You shouldn't speak that way about Evita,' he said, and there was something menacing about the softness of his intonation, and about the way that scar moved up and down his neck, caressing his Adam's apple with its memory of violence.

I guessed that Vicente had gone off the idea of seducing me.

Porteños' peculiar brand of unhappiness, their arrogance, their fixation on Europe were the butt of jokes all over South America. 'An Argentine is an Italian who speaks Spanish, and wants to be English,' was one joke and there were many others. 'How does an Argentine commit suicide?' a Peruvian asked me once, during a power-cut in the Andes. In the dark, I heard him almost weeping with laughter. 'He throws himself off his own ego.'

Where did the unhappiness start? For a long time I thought that it must be the legacy of the violence that had ravaged the country in the 1970s. But as I lived in Buenos Aires, breathed the disaffection myself, I began to feel that the melancholy extended much further back, that in fact it was as old as the country itself. Argentina had not been settled, as America had, by men and women with convictions and ideals, but by the poor, the homesick, the greedy. Thousands had come here to make money, and many had left, taking the money away with them. The violence that accompanied the early days of the republic had never been resolved. Rather than mix with the natives, as the newcomers had done in other Latin American countries, Argentines remained a predominantly European race. Most of the Indians had been exterminated in the desert campaign of the 1870s.

Even now, many *porteños* shunned a relationship to the continent in which they had been born. At one dinner-party, a wealthy woman with gold stilettos and silicon bosoms boasted of the 'purity' of her blood. 'I'm as European as you can get,' she told me. Her ancestors, some hundred years previously, would have collected a cash reward for every dead Indian – a set of severed ears or genitals was required as proof of the patriotic deed.

One morning, as I was returning home from two hours of queues, I was stopped by a young woman holding a microphone and accompanied by a cameraman. 'Do you believe in true love at first sight?' she asked. 'It's for a television show.'

She was wearing striped leggings and had wild curly hair and eyebrows that bounced up and down with her questions, perhaps with the aim of encouraging her interviewees. I hesitated. I wanted to match the enthusiasm of her leggings and her bouncing eyebrows, but instead I felt dejected by them. How could I believe in true love, when I had just been thinking that nothing in Argentina was really true?

'People don't always know what they mean by "true love",' I said finally. 'They might be confusing it with lust or idealism, or a fear of loneliness.'

At home some days later, it took me a few seconds to realise that the anxious foreigner on television, seriously expounding on the impossibility of true love, was actually myself. I looked pale and tearful. The research I had been doing on the disappeared and their missing children had drained me. A creeping claustrophobia had taken hold of me and I had begun to despise the country which, through its literature, had fascinated me since my schooldays. One evening, I wrote in my diary: 'in some places, every idiosyncratic goof is endearing. You feel affection for the noise, the grubby streets, the graffiti, the inefficiency of the bureaucrats. Here you hate them. Everything feels designed to frustrate. It seems that good intentions don't exist.'

CHAPTER FIVE

A Fear of Falling Buttocks

A FRIDAY AFTERNOON IN winter found me in the Confitería Ideal, a café, in the centre of Buenos Aires, that looked as old as the century. The great salon was like a ballroom in decay. Once wealthy socialites had come here to dance to European orchestras and there were still chandeliers and handsome mahogany panels lining the walls, but the mirrors were dappled by age and cheap electric fans had been fastened to the marble columns. In glass cabinets, silver tea-pots and champagne flutes were displayed like precious archaeological relics, among boxes of brightly wrapped sweets that looked like jewels.

As befitted a traditional Argentine café, the waiters were elderly – it was somehow disappointing to find one that was merely middle aged – and dressed in white jackets that had been starched and darned many times over the decades. Wearing the expression of dignified disapproval favoured by top establishments, they moved creakily among the tables, bearing pots of coffee to gossiping women with hair dyed gold. Conversations, especially gossip, were conducted in a low murmur at the Ideal, the ladies murmuring their scandals like a litany. On occasion, the reverential hush was such that it was disturbed only by the cranky working of electric fans and the distant rumble of underground trains below.

Yet there was evidence that the café was trying to recapture, if not the glamour, at least some of the lively attitude it had once had. On one side of the salon stood a second-hand electric organ, mounted on a low platform. An old man with hairs scraped across his gleaming pate came to sit at the organ every afternoon. For two hours, he electrocuted tangos. His awful renditions of Argentine classics were destined to offend only the salon's ghosts, for the golden-haired ladies, deep in adulteries and illegitimacies, were impervious to the music. A flame of rebellion must have fluttered in the little man's heart, because he occasionally sneaked muzak in among the tangos. No one was any the wiser. Whatever music he played sounded as if it belonged at the end of Brighton pier amid candyfloss and saucy postcards, not in this decaying ballroom at the end of the world.

The organist was playing 'I'm in Heaven', but I sat in the Confitería Ideal that afternoon with a sinking heart. I had an appointment to teach English conversation to Sylvia, an anorexic publicist in her forties. I hated teaching English, and I especially hated teaching it to Sylvia.

Since her husband had left her some years previously, Sylvia had been dwindling at a startling rate, but she still thought she was fat. She came to the classes straight from her psychoanalysis sessions, and made little distinction between the two. The main difference was that our hour was in English, and I earned considerably less for listening to her problems. Our conversations almost always followed the same lines. Sylvia would arrive late, apologise and say that this was because she was tired and she had a headache.

'I am a little sad,' she would say, 'because I am not in love.' An emerald engagement ring sparkled reproachfully from the wrong hand.

'Maybe love is not the answer,' I tried, in various versions. 'Love ties you down. When you're single you have the freedom to do more things.' She was never convinced.

I worried sometimes that Sylvia's English vocabulary was too much centred on love, food and headaches, but she would not be drawn on any other subject and, since her life revolved around the impossibility of the first two and the frequency of the third, anything else she might have learned would have been superfluous. The vocabulary she had was limited, but it was also highly detailed: she was proud to have learned and understood the different meanings and nuances of 'unhappy', 'sad', 'melancholy' and even 'glum'. Sylvia was fast becoming an expert on English words to do with woe.

Since she was also expert in *viveza criolla*, we often met in cafés that belonged to her clients, so that there was no bill to pay. From my point of view this was not necessarily a good arrangement. Sylvia had made it virtually a condition of our classes that I consume chocolate cake every time we met – thus she satisfied vicariously her longing for calories. In Buenos Aires, where image was so important, food was an essential weapon of psychological warfare among women and one which Sylvia used with particular virulence. When the food was free it was much harder to fend off the cake or whatever else she had in mind to fatten me with. If I refused to consume, she became quite agitated. 'But you must!' she would exclaim. 'Why not a little sandwich or a quiche? It's free! Why don't we share something?' At this point I usually gave in, even though I knew that she was bound to renege on the deal. Fortunately, when the food was to be paid for, Sylvia was much less insistent and, thankfully, she had no friends at the Ideal.

That afternoon Sylvia arrived late, as usual, and I rose to greet her. I asked how she was, dreading what was sure to be a long and laborious answer. Sylvia was presently being attended by three analysts simultaneously, but, instead of making her life easier, they had complicated it even more. I wondered if that was really the whole point of analysis – to cloud the outlook to such an extent that one could no longer discern the original problem. In that sense at least, the analysis was working, because Sylvia had stopped worrying about her life long ago; her main source of concern was the very nature and expense of her analysis. To start with, the psycho-triumvirate had allowed Sylvia to do publicity for them, instead of paying, but now they wanted cash, and lots of it. Unable to stump up what they demanded, Sylvia was accumulating a financial debt that seemed to outweigh any spiritual gain the twice-weekly sessions could provide. The analysts had suggested she ask her married lover to foot the bill, advice that seemed to be directly at odds with their role in fostering Sylvia's independence.

So, in answer to my question, Sylvia said: 'I am not very well, I am very *angustiada*. How do you say "angustia"?' She sat down and took out her vocabulary notebook, ready to add this new word to her gloomy collection. I noticed Sylvia's thin face fattened in the reflection of my metal coffee pot. Behind her on the pot one of the elderly waiters came creaking in our direction, upside down and expanding as he approached.

'The word's "anguish",' I said. 'But in English it's more serious – we use it for suffering that is really very bad indeed.' The only example that came immediately to mind was crucifixion. 'Perhaps what you want is something more like "miserable" or "upset". Have we done those?'

'No, no!' Sylvia was determined not to have her mood demoted. 'I *am* suffering really very bad indeed,' she insisted. 'I have very much anguish and, you know, I have gained one kilo.' She bowed her head and almost whispered this last shameful information, as if the ladies gossiping around us might seize on it as an addition to their litany of scandals.

'But it suits you. You look very well.'

'No, it's terrible, a terrible thing.'

'Well, I'm very sorry to hear that you're not happy,' I said, as briskly as I dared, because I did not feel equal to another discussion of Sylvia's problems. 'Look, I brought something that might cheer you up.'

As she ordered coffee, I took out a selection of articles from English newspapers and magazines which I had brought with me, thinking they might interest her and extend her vocabulary. We could either read them together now, I suggested, or Sylvia could take them home and we could discuss them in our conversation class the following week. I proposed that we might also go to see *Much Ado About Nothing*, which was currently playing in Argentine cinemas under the Spanish title *Much Noise, Few Nuts*. When her English improved a little, I had novels I could lend her. I found myself feeling suddenly quite positive about the challenge of improving Sylvia's English.

Sylvia accepted the articles and put them in her bag, but she made it clear that she was not remotely interested in them. In fact her eyes glazed over as I discussed the possibility of cinema trips and English literature. I was wondering aloud if she might take to Graham Greene, or Muriel Spark, when she leaned over and touched my arm.

'Do you want to be more thin?' she asked, with malicious feeling. It was a shot across the bows, and I found myself manoeuvred into a rapid, unconvincing defence.

'No I do not! I'm happy as I am, thank you!'

'Good!' Sylvia made a smile to convey that she did not believe me. She gave a patronising little shrug – 'if you are happy, it's fine' – and I felt a surge of hatred towards her. There had been no chocolate cake on hand today, so she was trying to beat me some other way. I pondered acts of violence that included taunting her about that extra kilo, the lack of a boyfriend. She would be easy to hurt.

'Actually we say "thinner", not "more thin",' I said, aware that this was not nearly revenge enough.

Sylvia removed her infuriating smile from me then and bestowed it on a little child vendor who had stopped at our table, and was winding something up with a look of intense concentration, as he had at all the other tables before us. Poor men, women and children circulated round the cafés of Buenos Aires selling all manner of curious objects – self-massaging devices or fondue sets – at suspiciously low prices.

'What have you got for us?' Sylvia asked the child.

'A toaster,' he said.

'A toaster?'

'A crazy toaster.'

The boy released a blue plastic box with yellow feet on to the table and the three of us watched as it waddled across the wooden surface – yellow smiling toast popping up and down – past Sylvia's coffee and towards her thin, bejewelled hand. The hand hovered spiderishly, then pounced on its Taiwanese prey.

'Nice,' said Sylvia. She handed the boy a dollar and dropped the toy into her handbag, where it paddled impotently against the leather until the cord ran out.

Of course I wanted to be thinner. Every woman in Buenos Aires, no matter her size, wanted to be thinner. Looks, but more particularly women's looks, were a persistent, urgent topic of conversation. Argentina spent more money on cosmetic surgery than almost any other country in the world and was fast developing the highest incidence of anorexia. Two-thirds of school girls had ambitions to become, not lawyers, doctors or scientists, but models – and this was somehow not felt to be a national disaster. When a German 'supermodel' visited Buenos Aires to promote lingerie, she was accorded more honours than a head of state, meeting the president twice and travelling around the city in a fleet of limousines, pursued by thousands of fans. Her thoughts on beauty and lingerie commanded front pages for five days.

Teenage models were the new stars of Argentine society. They danced tangos with the president, adorned the covers of magazines and had their pick of society's richest, most powerful men. Sometimes barely pubescent, they fluttered on the fringes of televised debates, giving inane but charming opinions on everything from industrial growth to astrology, which they often claimed to adore, for they were prone to adoring things. Weekly magazines devoted pages to models' philosophies of life. Graciela, a former *Playboy* centrefold, appeared in one volunteering an unusual hobby. 'Calculus is almost an addiction with me. I adore solving complex mathematical equations.' Later in the same interview she revealed: 'I'm a very genuine person. I feel at my most sincere during an orgasm.' Alongside the article there were pictures of Graciela looking very sincere in a gold-lamé bikini.

Image was master in Buenos Aires. 'One of the worst traits we inherited from the Italians is the compulsion to *fare bella figura*,' said Martín, who was actually one of the worst offenders. 'We direct all our efforts into the packaging, and ignore the contents.'

This was half true. Although men also spent over the odds on clothes and cosmetic surgery, in practice they could do whatever they liked; it was only unforgivable for a woman to age or grow fat. Female television presenters over a certain age – and there were precious few of them – wore long bleached hair and the fixed smiles of multiple face-lifts. Magazines imposed an aesthetic regime that was tyrannical. If a celebrity had taken too long to recover from a pregnancy or had allowed her buttocks to 'fall' – a phenomenon that fascinated and appalled *porteños* – she was chastised with a merciless close-up and a cutting editorial advising her to get in shape. Prime-time television entertainment included competitions in which men tried to guess a woman's vital statistics by running their hands over the contours of her body, or tested their skill at matching a row of women's barely covered buttocks to the correct faces. Real women were used in these contests. They never stopped smiling as the contestants squeezed and prodded them.

One stylish new chat show, broadcast every week from Miami, boasted an innovative slot: a weekly interview with a Hollywood has-been – say a Charlie's angel or an ex-TV cop – conducted in halting English, with subtitles. After the interview, the celebrity was always invited to watch a video of young models carrying out mundane activities in bikinis or mini-skirts, to a pop song. 'You wanna see chicks rollerskate?' the host purred at his surprised American guests. 'You wanna see chicks go shop?'

I thought that they looked less like chicks than ostriches, confused and rather stupid at the top of their long legs – but perhaps I was jealous. I was living in a country where breathtaking amounts of money and time were spent on hairdressers, clothes and beauty treatments, where falling buttocks were an issue of national debate. For the first time, I felt distinctly uneasy in my skin. I wondered if I should start having manicures or be more assiduous about waxing. My body was no longer private – it existed in a public domain to be commented on and scrutinised by people I did not know in the street.

The obsession with looks, many *porteños* agreed, made relationships problematic in Buenos Aires; the country's divorce rate was the highest in South America. One of the capital's dating agencies announced publicly that it was to close after five years' business had yielded only one marriage (and that was looking rocky). The agency's director appeared on television, exasperated by her failure. 'I've organised more than a thousand dates and only one of them came to fruition,' she told the reporter. 'Argentines don't know how to form proper relationships. The men want someone young and beautiful. The women all want money. Nobody's realistic.'

Women's magazines added to the confusion by offering disconcerting advice on how to hold on to your husband, or how to get more out of him – more money, for example. Once I discovered a list of suggestions 'to keep him interested' which included: 'changing the colour of your hair regularly – he likes variety; laughing at his jokes, even if you don't find them funny; winking at him – it makes him feel supported; never forgetting to pay attention to your looks'.

I saw no reason to change my hair-colour or laugh at dull jokes. I could not bring myself to take up winking, but certainly I was worried about my looks – should I pay more attention to them?

Raquel, who also wanted to be thinner, suggested we try a new concept in fitness: 'effortless exercise'. She knew of a salon fitted out with machines imported from the United States, and it belonged to a distant cousin, which meant that we would not have to pay to use them. Raquel claimed that all you did was lie on the machines while they worked different parts of your body. In a few weeks we would be thinner, miraculously.

We started going twice a week to the salon and learned to use all the machines. We were careful never to make any effort; the hum of the machines as they worked at our bodies was comforting and soporific and sometimes we even fell asleep on the machines as our legs were monotonously raised and lowered or our waists shuffled from side to side.

One afternoon I lay on a machine having my backside pummelled, to ward off the dreaded fall, while Raquel slumbered on the abdominals machine beside me. A svelte blonde, probably in her forties, entered the room, accompanied by one of the salon's assistants. The blonde was immaculately dressed in silver tights and a designer leotard it would have been reckless to sweat in. The couple were in mid-conversation, the blonde emphasising whatever point she was making by gesturing vigorously with her long fingernails, as if she were trying to dry the glossy red polish on them. As the assistant helped her on to one of the machines near me, the blonde said:

'Did I tell you I got a return flight to Miami out of him?'

'Are you serious? That's marvellous!'

'I'm going next month. He started off by suggesting we go halves on the flight, but I said, "Look, pay the whole thing or you can forget about seeing me again."'

Both the women laughed, as if this were a corny old trick, but one that worked surprisingly often. The blonde lay down and positioned her silver legs on to padded rests. She gave the red-taloned hands temporary respite on her stomach, though every so often they would be called on to illustrate a new grievance.

'I was quite hard on him,' she admitted, 'but that's because I've had enough of making do with whatever scraps he deigns to give me after she's got the best of everything.'

'Well, you deserve it, Manuela – you've been there for him for years, haven't you? Think of all those times he's been off with the wife and kids and you've been stuck at home, wondering if he's going to call.'

'He gave me spending money, too.'

'So he should.'

The machine was switched on and the blonde's legs started automatically to move up and down, so that she seemed to be striding towards the ceiling. Her unbending legs and the mass of false blonde hair reminded me of a Sindy doll I had once made stride around my bedroom in similar fashion.

'It's not as if I get that much from him – a dress here or there, or a little bit of money, and I have to pay the rent and clothes and the analyst.' The red-tipped fingers sprang to the cause of enumerating these expenses. 'My costs are high, you know. Sometimes I've waited for days for that bastard to call without hearing a single thing. Then he sweeps back in with a bunch of flowers as if nothing had happened. Honestly, I feel so much *bronca*, sometimes I wonder if I should give up on him and find someone of my own.'

'It's hard to find the right man, Manuela. You're probably better off making the most of the situation, so long as you don't let him take you for granted.'

'And I'm fond of him, that's the trouble. You can turn it up higher, Cristina.' The assistant obeyed and the machine responded with a more determined hum. The blonde's legs started to scissor rapidly. Light streaming in the window found her silver tights slicing through the air like blades.

'That's good,' she sighed. 'Good for the arse. I'm going to get another man in Miami and show that bastard.'

After a few weeks, Raquel's cousin told us that we would have to work harder if we were serious about improving our figures. The principle of effortless exercise, apparently, was not that one made no effort at all, but rather that less effort was necessary than in other activities. The cousin was obviously growing tired of providing free sessions. We stopped going after that.

Many women declared themselves grateful for men's approval of their looks in the street. 'I feel depressed if I walk two blocks without a peep from anyone,' said a woman on the radio. I hated the comments, the way men leaned into my space and whispered their relish of my anatomy. It was even worse when they bypassed my face and addressed themselves directly to my chest. Often the men were old enough to have been somebody's grandfather, if not mine. I tried to be oblivious to them, but the anticipation of comments made me self-conscious. Once I had strolled, now annoyance made me strut – in fact I broke a heel that way. Sometimes I was noisy in the street, countering the suggestions with a volley of tuttings and shushings. In a bad mood, I rounded on the lechers and made offensive remarks about their own bodies. When I primly informed a man with a goitre that it was rude to talk to strangers, his eyebrows scuttled up his forehead like grubbing insects. 'We won't need to talk in bed, darling.'

One morning I was waiting to cross the road to the laundrette, when a well-dressed man standing a few yards away smiled at me and raised a hand in greeting. I smiled back, thinking he must be someone I had interviewed. He had the look of a political analyst, or an economist. The man approached me and I saw that I would have to forfeit my chance to cross the road.

'Hello,' he said. 'Have you been shopping?' He smiled towards the plastic bags I was carrying.

'No, I'm on my way to the laundrette.' I was also taking the shoe with the broken heel to be mended.

'Where are you from, señorita?'

I realised then that I did not know the man after all, and now I was obliged to have some sort of conversation when I least wanted one. He was wearing a dark-green worsted suit and his thinning hair was swept off a broad forehead that was laid out with fine lines like puppet-wires. I could see how the lines worked to lift and move different parts of his face. Since his eyes were very dark, they were bound to look penetrating, and I was suddenly uneasily aware of my untidiness. Most of my wardrobe was in the bags and I was wearing a motley assortment of the last clean clothes left to me. It was a fair bet that my hair was unbrushed.

'I'm from Britain.'

'Ah.' The man's eyes lit up. Being British was a shamefully easy way to impress people. He made the usual remarks about the London smog and the Royal Family and threw in a joke about the manliness of Margaret Thatcher. I made my accustomed responses to the first two, and laughed at the joke, which I had heard before. Meanwhile, I missed more opportunities to cross the road.

When the joke had run its course, the man pondered me for a second or two, then he said, 'Look, I'm too old to have an affair now, but how about a coffee?'

'No, thank you,' I said automatically. 'I should get on with my things.' Seconds later it struck me that what the man had said was offensive, but I was unsure which part of the equation dishonoured me more: his having considered an affair with me, or his having ruled it out in favour of coffee.

'That's a shame,' said the man. He stroked his chin thoughtfully while the dark eyes tried to make sense of me. I was a foreigner, exotic, untidy, not right for an affair perhaps, but Buenos Aires worked on contacts, and I might be useful to him at a later date. At any rate, he was looking for a longer association than this roadside encounter allowed. Meanwhile, all I wanted was to get to the laundrette. Was there any reason, I wondered, why I should stand about being polite to someone who had so rudely unpropositioned me? I could feel my clothes writhing in the bags; my hair, I remembered now, was not only unbrushed, but dirty.

'Perhaps you would like to dance a tango instead?' the man said finally. 'I go to the same tango hall every Friday, I'd be delighted to see you there.' He jotted down the address on a card and handed it to me. 'No strings attached,' he said, but I saw those puppet wires pull his mouth into a particular smile.

The old tango hall was just off Avenida Corrientes, 'the street that never sleeps'. A sign outside the hall forbade jeans and required jackets, and a tussle of wrongly dressed men hung around the doorman remonstrating about this. Inside, the lights were dimmed to a suggestive red and the words 'Salón Argentina – not just a place, but somewhere to make friends' were fading over the stage. A three-piece band tackled songs of love, misery and death.

It was only nine o'clock, but there were already nearly a hundred people in the hall, maybe twenty of them dancing. I sat watching the dancers moving under the lights and saw that any one of them might have found room in a fashionable South American novel. A thin man with a pale, suffering face was like the bridegroom who goes mad with grief in Gabriel García Márquez's *Chronicle of a Death Foretold*. He gripped his woman as if she were his last resort, his pallid cheek pressed hard against her forehead, his tousled hair seeking to entwine itself with hers. Their movement across the floor was fluid, though punctuated by dramatic turns and complicated steps; it looked as if the dance really had meaning for them.

Following in their wake, a large woman with mooning buttocks let herself be led a more perfunctory dance by a short man in whom she was careful not to show the slightest interest, perhaps because he was her husband. The man seemed to grimace with the effort of moving and turning his large partner, or else with the melancholy of the lyrics and the music. He had a rather absurd moustache and I decided that he reminded me of the scriptwriter in the novel by Mario Vargas Llosa. All the dancers wore the unhappy expression that was essential to a tango attitude. As the Argentine novelist Ernesto Sábato once wrote, 'only gringos dance tango for fun.'

I had heard it said that tango was the only dance in the world not intended to express joy. Danced properly, it should be as passionate, yet as loveless as a one-night stand. While the dancers' legs and hips engaged in erotic intertwining, the upper bodies kept a cool distance. The heads touched, but in such a way that made eye contact impossible. Dancers did not smile at each other or make small talk; it was wrong to talk about the weather or offer your partner a drink. A man invited a woman to dance simply by nodding at her; she assented grimly and, after their brief, unhappy tryst, the dancers returned to separate tables. Some tango halls charged ten dollars for the pleasure of such pain.

I had come out that night with an English friend, a mysterious girl whose determination to escape an unhappy love affair in London had brought her here, to the world's end. She accepted, with a strange fatalism, that she would spend the rest of her life in Argentina, even though her family wrote regularly begging her to return and she had no reason to cross them. ' "Forever" was the first word I learned to say in Spanish,' she once told me. It must have been a very unhappy love affair.

Emma was good at tango, easily mustering the melancholy necessary to be convincing. Pressing her smooth cheek against the faces offered by numerous partners, she often closed her eyes as she danced, and allowed a shadow of torment to drift across her face. Perhaps she remembered her old terraced home in London, or the lover who had caused her to leave it. Emma was good at tango because it was invented for people like her: she was that most traditional and typical of *porteños* – an ambivalent immigrant.

The tango started life as a symptom of a city with growing pains. A hybrid of sailor's song and Italian dance tune played on a German accordion, the genre was born in the ports of Buenos Aires around 1880 when the city was still a frontier town and more than half its inhabitants were new arrivals from the poorest parts of Europe. Over the next forty years, the population of Buenos Aires grew rapidly, from 500,000 to three million, as men and women flocked to 'make America'. A whole Spanish village had made the journey. But the dream of easy money proved elusive for many of them. Tango became the anthem of a generation of homesick and sometimes desperate immigrants. Usually set in Buenos Aires, the songs always yearned for a happier past. Many of them were addressed to the singer's mother or an ex-lover. A few were reserved for fallen women, and there was special opprobrium for women who had abandoned their families and their class to be lured away by the high life, or *jailiefe*, as the lyrics had it. Often the sentiment was desperate, suicidal.

Soon after the haunting music was invented, it was accompanied by a strange dance which, in view of the shortage of women at the time, men danced with each other – hence the wary physicality of some movements. By the turn of the century, the city's brothels had started hiring out their women as dance-partners by the hour, but tango's popularity was still restricted to sailors, low-lifers and small-time assassins. At the city's margins, tango sessions went on until dawn, often ending in knife-fights and murder. 'Perhaps tango's real purpose is to give Argentina the certainty of having once been valiant,' Borges wrote.

At the end of the 1920s, the American poet Waldo Frank described his own experiences of tango valour in *América Hispana*:

> The town keeps its violence, which is also of the pampa, scabbarded in grace. To find it naked, go into the suburbs, anodyne as a glass of lukewarm water. Behind the pasty villas and the grass-plots, you may come upon a gigantic barn with soldiers at the door. As you step in, they bow politely, ask if you are armed and before you can answer, frisk you for weapons. The hall is aglare with yellow varnish; pulsant with men and women massed in the bonds of the tango. The glare winks out; on a dark wall a motion picture gives cascading glimpses of naked women and men in sexual union. The dancing maze throbs on. Violins, harmonicas, flutes, weave the tango music, interminable as the generations, pulsant, monotonous, delicious as the play of sex. There are many doors on the long walls, and in those that are open stand women fastening their shifts, men buttoning their trousers ... So intense is the current within the man and the woman, that it leaps the air and copulates them.

No wonder the Vatican wanted it banned, and Queen Mary refused to attend London dances where the tango was to feature. But avant-garde Europeans fell in love with a less pornographic version of the dance and, since anything that was fashionable in Europe was slavishly imitated in Buenos Aires, upper-class Argentines vowed to love it too. By the 1930s tango had reached beyond the low-lifers and brothels of Buenos Aires to become high fashion. 'I used to go straight out to the dance halls after work, come home in the morning and have a quick nap before working again,' said Juan, who had arrived from Spain in 1930, aged fifteen, and still worked in one of the cafés on my block. 'That was the most marvellous time in the history of Buenos Aires.'

Soon tango singers were converted into filmstars and idols, the most famous of them Carlos Gardel, whose death in an air crash in 1935 brought Buenos Aires to a standstill. Gardel's portrait still adorned the capital's bars and a giant version of it smiled down on his street, the Avenida Corrientes. The life-size statue at his tomb was never without flowers or a cigarette placed tenderly between the waiting fingers of his left hand. His name was a benchmark – if you wanted to praise someone you compared him to the legendary singer. Equally, you could cut someone down to size with a curt 'He's no Gardel.'

It was often wrily observed that the anxieties dealt with in the early tangos – corruption, unemployment and injustice – were as relevant now as they had been in the tango's heyday. 'People who loved tango in the 1930s mostly lived in great financial straits,' a radio producer at FM Tango told me. 'The economic crisis we're experiencing now is very similar, except that nowadays the poor are even poorer. They still find a reflection of their problems in tangos. You know, Argentines can listen to the national anthem and it doesn't mean a thing to them, but if they hear tango, tears start pouring down their cheeks.'

Whether the tango would live, die or tragically pine away was a question frequently debated over *cafecito* or cognac. The genre was regularly dubbed the true expression of the Argentine soul, but it seemed to me that it was essentially about the impossibility of human contact at anything other than a violent level. Was the Argentine soul really such a dark and lonely place? Many people told me that it was.

At the Salón Argentina, the melancholic warmth exhaled by the musicians and dancers met a cold, specific tension as it seeped into the darker regions beyond the red lights. The tables clustered around the dance-floor were mostly occupied by solitary women, waiting to be invited to dance. The men who might invite them lurked at the back of the hall, brooding on the dancers and on their chances. While the waiting women inspected their hands nervously or toyed with glasses of Coca-Cola, men rolled whisky around their mouths. Women held on tight to their handbags. I saw a man make his way to the lavatory holding a bottle of deodorant and a woman discreetly gauge the exposure of her cleavage. It was perfectly obvious that Salón Argentina was a place to make more than friends. The waiting men watched the scene before them like predators, while the waiting women wore expressions of indignation, as though they were anticipating an improper suggestion. Surely they were, for an invitation to dance the tango *was* an improper suggestion, an insinuation of sex or even a prelude to it. 'Vertical sex', someone had called it. On Friday nights in Buenos Aires, couples queued in the street for an hour of the real, horizontal stuff in one of the city's many 'transitory hostels'. I had seen the couples waiting patiently, the red light reflected in their faces. Having spent all day queuing for money, for food or to pay bills, perhaps it seemed only natural to them to queue again for sex.

Close to my table, an unshaven man leaned against a marble column and watched the dancers with the sardonic half-smile of a Graham Greene character. I decided that he was the Honorary Consul, looking for solace in whisky and a woman. His eyes were fixed on one pair of dancers and I followed them to an unusual couple who were dominating the dance-floor with their erotic movement. The man was dark-skinned with brilliantined hair and he wore the cheaply respectable suit of a salesman. His partner was a punkish blonde clad in a tight leather outfit that was slit all the way up one leg. Their dancing required frequent exposure of the woman's thigh as she wrapped it copulatively around her partner's waist. Their hips sought engagement, but both of them frowned, as if such intimate contact caused them intellectual distaste, as well as physical pleasure. They only ever danced together, but they always sat apart between dances and I never saw them exchange a word.

While Emma glided tragically round the room with a handsome architect, I danced with his friend, a short man and a profuse sweater. I tried not to mind that his forehead was leaving its sticky imprint on my hair. My partner was a psychoanalyst, but he worked only with the people from shanty towns. 'The poor also have souls,' he told me defensively, as if I had suggested that they might not. 'They also know what it is to feel *angustiados*, to feel that life has no meaning.'

The psychoanalyst was light on his feet, effecting a dextrous tip-toe to the music that I could only follow awkwardly. In tango, a man determines his partner's next step by pressing her back accordingly with his right hand. The psychoanalyst kept stabbing his finger under my shoulder blade, but I did not always understand the instruction. 'I've only danced tango once before,' I confessed. 'I can tell,' he said rudely, and I found myself resenting his sticky forehead much more after that.

I had danced with two more short, fat men, both also efficient sweaters, before I saw that the elegant man, the man who had offered me coffee in place of romance, was standing at the bar looking on with amusement. He smiled as I approached with Emma.

'You brought protection!'

'My mother warned me never to dance the tango with strange men,' I said. I introduced Emma, who accepted the offer of a drink and made some brief, enigmatic small talk before returning to her architect. Then the man said, 'Shall I show you how to dance?'

He led me back on to the dance-floor beneath the suggestive red lights.

'If you really want to learn tango, first of all remember to do as you're told. In the real world, women rule, but here men give the orders. We like to fantasise that we're important for a couple of hours.'

We circled the dance floor a couple of times, until I began to get the hang of the basic steps. The man smelled of a smart office, of an expensive cologne defused by air-conditioning, of business deals briskly executed.

'Do you come here every week?' I asked.

'Just about.'

'Why do you dance the tango? Be warned that I may quote you.'

'Because I am Argentine, and tango is the expression of the Argentine soul,' said the elegant man. 'How's that?'

'It's a good quote,' I agreed, 'but I thought the tango was invented by criminals and homesick sailors.'

He smiled. 'To be Argentine is to be homesick, necessarily. We're all harking back to something.'

'Where's home?'

'Who knows? It's in the villages of southern Italy or northern Spain, the slums of Paris and Milan. Or perhaps it never existed. It could be a figment of the collective imagination. Try to relax your body more and think about what you're doing without looking at your feet.'

'And Argentines are all criminals?'

He laughed. 'Not criminals, but we're not great law-abiders, either. Do you know the word *chanta*?'

I did know it; it was a cherished word in the *porteño* vocabulary, meaning a fraud, a chancer. Politicians and businessmen were constantly referred to as *chantas*. Maradona was admired as a *chanta*. General Perón, someone once told me, was both the greatest Argentine and the greatest *chanta*.

'We're all *chantas*,' said my dance partner. 'We're all opportunists. Are you married, by the way?'

'Nearly,' I said, 'but you're too old for affairs anyway.' He laughed again and pulled me closer, his right hand tucked under my arm, so that my face was almost resting on the lapel of his worsted suit. Softly, he sang some of the lyrics to the music that was being played.

'The world is and always has been a pigsty, / In 510 and 2000 as well, / There were always crooks, schemers and fraudsters, / Happy and embittered men, idealism and lies. / But that the twentieth century is a display of insolent evil, / Nobody can deny.'

'Are all Argentines unhappy, then?' I said.

'What a thing to ask,' he murmured into my hair. 'Can't you see it in their faces?'

I had seen their faces and, strangely enough, I had seen some of the original faces, some of the very first people to emigrate to Buenos Aires and be unhappy there. A couple of weeks previously I had accompanied a friend to the morgue. Her uncle had died, and she had to make a lengthy enquiry about the corpse, which he had wanted donated to medicine. I waited for her in a wood-lined anteroom with deep leather armchairs and large oil paintings of Roman ruins.

'This is a beautiful room,' I observed to a porter who was standing nearby.

A slow smile stretched the porter's lips against his yellowing teeth. 'You wouldn't think it was so beautiful if you could see what was on the other side of this door.'

'Why? What's there?'

It was a great, wooden door, about ten feet high with a brass plaque I guessed was polished daily. Argentina was still the sort of 'developing' country where legions of public workers were employed to keep things clean. Once it had acquired First World status, presumably it would get dirty. The shining plaque simply read 'Museo'.

'The Museum of the Morgue,' said the man, with admirable drama. 'It's full of dead people who died in funny ways. Casualties of history you might call them. There are all sort of curiosities.'

He glanced towards the administrative office and lowered his voice. 'I'm not supposed to, but I'll let you inside if you like. It's interesting.'

'I don't know . . .'

'You have to be psychologically prepared for it, mind. Even final-year medical students faint in there sometimes.'

I hesitated, then shook my head – I was not at all sure that I was psychologically prepared. But the closed door with its shining brass plaque was intriguing, and my friend was taking her time over her uncle's corpse. The man kept smiling his lugubrious invitation with a persistence that obliged me to accept it.

'Maybe I'll have a quick look,' I conceded.

'You're psychologically prepared?'

'Well, I think so.'

At first, when the porter unlocked the door, and I saw the rows of pale human heads, arms and legs suspended in glass cases, I felt a sympathetic draining of my own blood. Then my body found a quick resilience and – egged on by the smiling porter – I stepped through the great doorway into an airless room. The door closed behind me and I was suddenly confronted by dozens of severed heads, floating in rows – a chorus of groaners. The eyelids were closed as if in sleep; they must have been eyeless. Their hair stuck up, like tufty clumps of algae, in the formaldehyde.

The heads all belonged to men who had died violently in the first decades of the century. Some had been murdered: shot or stabbed by other men, or by the police. Many had taken their own lives and three of the men still wore the knotted ropes that had killed them. Some of the faces gasped at the shock of their death, as if they had been frozen at the very moment a promising robbery went wrong. Others bore expressions of sleepy relief; here, finally, was the peace they had been looking for, the solution the *tangueros* sang about. Almost all the men were young immigrants. After visiting Argentina in the 1940s, the Spanish philosopher José Ortega y Gasset wrote that 'Argentine *tristeza* is of so elementary, nay massive a power-fulness, that it at once conquers any sensitive newcomer; I know of many who at first harboured thoughts of suicide for a whole week.'

Under every head, a typed card gave a brief summary of its truncated life: the man's country of origin, the year of his immigration, the date and cause of his death. A Czech sailor had been decapitated by a train. A Polish farm labourer was killed by a bullet to the brain. Among the criminals there was a head belonging to El Pibe Cabeza, a famous delinquent who led a band of murderers in the 1930s. His nickname, ironically, was 'Head', 'probably because he had a large head, or because he was known to be intelligent' suggested the typed information – with generous ambivalence, because Cabeza's head was as big as a pumpkin and wore an expression of irredeemable stupidity. Alongside it, a yellow cutting from a contemporary newspaper detailed Cabeza's gruesome crimes under the heading 'He Was Once a Hairdresser'. Now he was only a head. He was reduced to his nickname.

Next to Cabeza was an Italian who had arrived at the start of the century and worked as a knife-grinder. He had killed four babies borne him by different lovers before the police put a violent end to him. The expression on the man's face was terrifying, he looked enraged by his own assassination. Another case made grisly exhibition of the Italian's home-made tattoos, on pieces of skin taken from his arms and chest. One honoured General Perón. Another showed a couple dancing tango and another a man sodomising a crawling woman. Perón, tango and sodomy were the things that mattered most to this knife-grinder, who had travelled halfway across the world looking for riches. Dangling in a box beneath the man's head was his penis, and perhaps this undignified juxtaposition explained his outraged expression. He had tattooed his penis, 'For you'.

Elsewhere in the museum, there was a strangled seamstress and a domestic servant whose jealous husband had cut her throat with a shaving knife. Generally, the women in the museum were represented not by their heads but by their breasts and genitalia, for that was mostly where they had been attacked. The chest of a maid, stabbed nine times by her jealous husband in 1936, was displayed with the dagger still protruding from the ninth wound. Other women, pregnant or destitute, had taken cyanide. They were washerwomen and domestic servants, come to Argentina from Spain, Germany, the further reaches of Eastern Europe.

I was thankful that the different parts of an Italian lady, expertly dismembered by her husband, had been copied in wax for the purposes of the exhibition. Even without the evidence of flesh, I could see that she had been a very fat woman. Her big breasts sloped lazily away from her sternum and it looked as though her buttocks had not just fallen, but fallen quite a distance; she would have got short shrift from the style pages of an Argentine magazine. There was a photograph of the woman which had been taken soon after her immigration and a few years before she had died. There she stood, all of a solid piece, on the steps by the monument to San Martín, the liberator and hero of her adoptive country. She wore a little black hat, a fur jacket and some modest jewellery, and the woman smiled broadly, as if her luck had turned; she was positive about the new life that awaited her in Argentina. She was not to know that she would one day be a monument herself, her naked body reproduced to make a point about cruelty and despair in the New World.

That photograph, with its evocation of hope and humanity, did more to upset me than the chorus of groaning heads, and I decided then that I had seen enough. Back in the anteroom I sank into one of the deep leather armchairs.

'Did you get a shock?' asked the porter hopefully. 'You look a little pale, are you feeling ill?'

'I feel more sad than ill,' I said.

'Sad?' The porter seemed disappointed. 'Why?'

'To think that those people came all this way, and that things didn't work out for them.'

CHAPTER SIX

Evita Aflame

I WAS USED TO the noises of protest, the scare-rhythms that could quickly grow out of a din of drums, shouts and whistles – and yet I had never witnessed anything quite like this. It was a winter's night and another *sudestada* was going to town on Buenos Aires. At the margins of the city, shanty houses collapsed like flimsy excuses. Telephone poles came crashing down and litter, caught in the embrace of loose newspaper pages, rolled down the avenues like tumbleweed. Answering the call of one of the convocatory posters that sprang up overnight on the city's walls, I had battled through the wind and rain to an old theatre on the Avenida Corrientes. Now, with a curious detachment, I was watching a thousand people work themselves into a frenzy.

It was like being celibate at an orgy. A vast noise arose from various sections of the theatre, creating a blur of sound of which my ears could sometimes make only a ringing nonsense. The balcony, where I was standing, threatened to buckle under a pounding of synchronised stamping. Beneath me in the stalls was a swelling sea of heads, from which fists periodically leaped like jumping fish. I had the impression of a funeral party straying into a carnival because some of the people who were standing on the seats and jostling in the aisles cried and shouted, while others sang and blew whistles. A three-man jazz band which had been playing traditional Peronist dirges broke suddenly into 'Hello Dolly'. Upstairs, encouraged by their own impact on the shaking surroundings, the stamping women were shouting the Peronist Women's anthem with a red-faced determination. I tested the floor's resilience under my feet, and resolved to keep close to the wall.

At the front of the balcony, a few feet in front of me, a woman with a tear-soaked face stood alone, shaking her fist at the ceiling. She was ship-shaped, her long torso rising out of an ample belly that curved like a prow to her navel. The woman looked ready to launch herself over the balustrade into the sea of shouters downstairs, leaving behind her the shopping bag with vegetables, bread, two-for-one shampoos – everyday objects that were out of place in this otherworldly atmosphere. How had she reached such a level of distress? I wondered if she had just been shopping and decided to step off the street into this old theatre to scream for a hour before going home to make dinner for her husband. Such an effortless climb to hysteria was almost enviable. Curious, I tested a scream at the back of my throat – but it was not something I would confidently produce.

The noise was dramatic and insistent and the Peronist Women's Committee, which had organised this event, seemed powerless either to quieten it or to make their own mark on it. On stage, a smartly suited politician tried to make an announcement, but the shouters and the jazz band would not let her speak. She fiddled with a microphone, mouth opening and closing pointlessly, gestured angrily at the jazz men – who were too involved in 'Hello Dolly' to pay attention – and returned to her seat. Then an older woman, severely attired, walked to the front of the stage, fiddled more effectively with the microphone and roared into it:

'Comrades! Can we please have some quiet? Remember that this is a sad day, not one for celebrations. Perhaps our friends in the band could also bear that in mind, and search their repertoire for some rather more respectful music.'

At that, the jazzmen sulkily left off 'Dolly' and reapplied themselves to dirges. The drum took up a funereal beat.

It was 26 July and a day for sound and fury. After all, this was the day Evita died.

Once she had calmed the crowd, the speaker announced that there was going to be a short film, and a cinema screen dropped from the ceiling. There followed a projection of the famous grainy images every Argentine knew, blown now to gigantic proportions: here was the youthful Evita on the balcony of the Casa Rosada, both fists raised in a familiar gesture of aggression that was excitingly at odds with her elegant clothes and chignon. Here she was exhorting her people to 'fight to the death for Perón'. Here she was, much frailer, dying of uterine cancer at only thirty-three, weeping in front of a crowd of thousands. Her voice, vanquished by pain and grief, was barely intelligible:

> 'All that I have, I have in my heart, it hurts my soul, it hurts my flesh and it burns on my nerves, and that it is my love for the people and for Perón. And I thank you, my General, for having taught me to know that love and value it. Were the people to ask me for my life, I would give it to them singing, for the happiness of one *descamisado* is worth more than my life.'

At that moment, the tear-stained woman at the front of the balcony cried into the hushed air of the theatre: 'But, Evita, you never died, you're immortal!' and a din of shouting arose again from the stalls. 'Goddess!' 'Evita lives!' The women around me took up their stamping with renewed enthusiasm. Out of the confusion grew a chant; it started somewhere at the back of the stalls and at first I could not understand what was being said, but within seconds the chant had grown to encompass the whole theatre. Everyone was shouting, 'Se siente, se siente, Evita está presente.' 'We feel it, we feel it, Evita is present.'

The chant grew in volume and fervour and, up on the screen, Evita rippled slightly, as though moved by the breath of collective incantation. The giant, hollow face was frozen in an expression of absolute devastation. *Se siente, se siente, Evita está presente!* The shouting bound me to the screen and the giant face, perhaps the most potent image of violence and anguish I had ever seen, was mesmerising. Part of me wanted to fight the crowd's impetus and find my own control, yet my body acceded to the rhythms of voice and drum, the reverberations of floor and walls. The moment was both exhilarating and chilling. I wanted to chant too; I wanted to join in stamping down the balcony.

Looking around me, at the expressions of rage, passion and grief, it was possible to believe that Evita was indeed present that night.

All Evita ever wanted was to burn. Reading her books, watching her speeches in a dusty projection room at the National Archive, I was fascinated to see how often she made reference to fire. 'It is well worth burning up our lives, if the fruit is the peace and happiness of the world,' she reminded the delegates at a pan-American Conference on Welfare, 'even if this fruit ripens when we have disappeared.' Evita burned at the injustice of poverty, she burned with love for the *descamisados* or with hatred for the wealthy and she blazed through her own, short life, working long hours and barely sleeping, evading the doctors who might have cured her cancer.

Perhaps her cancer fed the flames, for, as she neared death, Evita's evocations of fire grew more urgent. She invoked obsessively the need 'to burn with fanaticism', telling a group of Peronist governors, 'those who believe in sweetness and love forget that Christ said "I have come to earth to bring fire, so that it may burn more" '. In the Plaza de Mayo she incited her followers to take up arms against the 'Oligarchy', the wealthy landowners she loathed. 'Shall we burn down the Barrio Norte?' she asked the thousands beneath the balcony. 'Shall I give you fire?'

Twenty years after Evita's death, her sister Erminda thought she could still detect a flickering in the face that was 'so tired of being dead'. In a poignant elegy to Evita's humiliated, battered body she wrote: 'I know that beneath your resting eyelids there is a fire that refuses to be extinguished.'

Why would anyone want to burn so much?

'If you could have seen her make just one of those tremendous, improvised speeches, you would have been amazed,' said writer María Luisa Rubertino. 'It was like watching a gun being fired. She used her body as a weapon and each word was a bullet.'

María Luisa and I met occasionally for tea and sandwiches at the Society of Authors, a kind of sanctuary around which elderly writers moved slowly, like zoological specimens waiting to be fed. The Society was in the Barrio Norte, that smart neighbourhood Evita had wanted to set alight.

'Do you think she really felt the powerful emotions she talked about, or was the rhetoric for the sake of the crowd?' I asked. 'She could just have been using the language to rouse people and secure their support for Perón.'

'No, I think she felt the passions so profoundly that they literally consumed her.'

María Luisa had researched Evita's life – even visiting the dusty pampa town where she was born in 1919 – for her play *Compañera*, or 'Comrade'. Out of loyalty, I had been to see *Compañera* twice. It was a low-budget production, miserably attended, in which abundant shouting and fist-waving were used to make up for a small cast. Evita's death-throes, which seemed to take even longer the second time I saw them, involved a prodigious production of tears and mucus. 'Don't let me die!' she wept in Perón's arms. 'I want to live for ever!' At the end of the performance the dozen or so of us in the audience followed the example of the cast, endeavouring to applaud for twice our number.

One afternoon, María Luisa told me of a theory she hardly dared advance to the really fervent Peronists.

'I'm sure that Evita could have saved herself,' she said. 'Her cancer was diagnosed early enough to operate and her mother had been cured of the same illness. But she made a decision to "burn up" her life, to achieve in seven years what most people take twenty years to do. I think she saw that there was an opportunity to turn herself into a legend, and she seized on it.'

'But did she sacrifice herself for Perón, or for her own hereafter?'

A door behind me swung open on to a symphony of kitchen noises, and a large serving woman came out to place our sandwiches and coffee before us with an irritated clatter. Inhibited by the interruption, María Luisa did not quite answer my question but, lowering her voice, she said:

'Did you know she was the same age as Christ when she died?'

Curiously, Juan Perón's first impressions of Evita were also of a woman who burned. In a memoir written from exile, he recalled meeting Eva Duarte at a fund-raising event for the city of San Juan, which had been devastated by an earthquake. It was 1944, Perón was minister for labour and a politician whose ambitions were increasingly reckoned by his superiors to be dangerous. Evita was a twenty-four-year-old actress popular for her work in radio soap operas. Not a star, but perhaps a starlet, she was well enough known to pout on magazine covers and for there to be public interest in her romantic life. For the sake of the gossip columns she invented high-class hobbies such as tennis and swimming, but privately she was already leaning towards socialism. Decades later, the words Perón remembered as being Evita's first were all too characteristic: 'We have to get money from those who have it.' He recalled a young woman whose anxious determination showed in her constant wring-ing of reddened hands. 'I was quite subdued by the force of her voice and her look,' he wrote. 'Eva was pale but when she spoke her face seemed to catch fire.'

To the shirtless masses, Evita's climb from provincial poverty to president's wife exemplified the new possibilities of the worker under Perón. She was blonde and beautiful, decked in fabulous jewels and clothes from Parisian fashion houses. She was daring, too, moving in with Perón at a time when cohabitation was deemed exceptionally shocking (Peronist supporters used to stand outside their apartment shouting 'Get married!'). Heedless of etiquette, Evita received guests in her pyjamas and gave them tins to eat out of, in place of meals.

Four months after their marriage, Perón became president and Evita relinquished her acting career for a greater stage and a much wider audience. Everything she did or said from now onwards would be destined to elevate her husband. In 'My Life's Cause', even her childhood memories were marshalled to the praise of the Peronist revolution. 'Perón is everything and I am nothing,' she repeated monotonously, 'nothing I have, nothing I am, nothing I think is mine; it all belongs to Perón.' And she would ask nothing of history for herself, other than a footnote in the glorious chapter that would surely be awarded Perón. 'As far as I am concerned, and I have analysed the subject in depth, Perón is perfect.'

Evita cast herself in the role of Christ, and Perón was the God whose message she sought to interpret for the masses. 'Sometimes I think that Perón has ceased to be an ordinary man and become an ideal incarnate,' she told one group of workers, and another, 'Perón is everything and the rest of us are an astronomical distance away from the leader of the nation.' The general, who had prided himself on his human touch, was now rendered awesome by his wife. There was a castrating quality about such adulation and some evidence suggested that Perón actually asked her to tone down the praise. Even so, a recording of one of her final speeches showed Evita promising to wreak bloody revenge on Perón's enemies while the leader himself stood meekly beside his wife in a white shirt and bow-tie, like a fat boy at a children's party. Meanwhile, Evita reserved for herself the much more sympathetic role of people's friend. Christlike, she offered herself as a 'bridge of love' between the people and the astronomically distant Perón.

Even in private, Evita's praise of her husband was constant and strenuous. 'I love you so much that what I feel for you is a kind of idolatry,' she wrote, after leaving on a state tour of European countries in 1949. The general never showed signs of loving her as much.

Although Evita held no official position in Perón's government, he awarded her a far-reaching, unchecked power. She was to be his link with the workers. At her office in the Ministry of Labour, the twenty-six-year-old arbitrated over industrial disputes and heard individual workers' grievances. At first only union members were given an audience, but later the rumour spread in Buenos Aires that the president's wife was willing to help any *descamisado* who had a problem, whether it was to do with work or not. Hundreds, then thousands of poor people started coming to the Ministry to tell Evita of their illnesses, their inadequate housing, their joblessness. Miraculously, in this bureaucratic country, Evita conjured up instant solutions. Jobs were found, planes were chartered to bring sick children to Buenos Aires. Packages of food and medicine were dispatched around the country.

In 1948, by which time Evita was receiving several thousand requests for help a day, her haphazard charity was reborn as the Eva Perón Foundation, a welfare organisation to be financed by government and union donations. Her daily contact with the poor remained undiminished. Argentines from all over the country beat a path to the Ministry of Labour, where their most common requests were for jobs, sewing machines and dentures. 'Argentines smile with none of the inferiority complexes of the downtrodden,' Evita boasted. She encouraged the *descamisados* to be bold in their requests, and, even then, she gave them more than they dared ask for. Delighted families left the Ministry with promises of new beds, new houses, food, clothes, spectacles and toys for the children. No one went away without money, and when she had no cash to hand Evita gave away pieces of her jewellery. She gave little thought to budgets, but Argentina was rich enough to foot the bill. The post-war years had brought booming exports and the country was experiencing a surge in prosperity. Few suspected, then, that the money would run out. For the moment, Perón's New Argentina was there for the asking.

Thanks to the Foundation, new hospitals and schools sprang up around the country, as well as hostels for single mothers and orphanages. A model workers' neighbourhood was built with the latest materials on the outskirts of Buenos Aires, and on the Avenida de Mayo there was a home for young women coming to work alone in the city, as Evita had once done. The Foundation provided free lunches for workers, cheap food stores and bargain funerals.

Evita was also keen to support the arts – so long as they supported Peronism. Historian Fermín Chávez belonged to a group of poets who met her every week for supper at the hostel on Avenida de Mayo. 'She was quite extraordinary, always beautiful and lively, even though we never saw her before midnight,' he told me, in a sitting room nostalgic with mementoes. The men took it in turns to read their poems to Evita, which were always paeans to her beauty and kindness, though she did not demand poems about herself, Fermín insisted: 'It just seemed the natural thing to do.'

The millions of people who benefited from her largesse would regard Evita for ever as a saint, as would their children and grand-children, but what the *descamisados* gave her in return was greater still, for she was quite desperate to be loved. Evita's determination never to let a child go without a toy nor a leper without a kiss was not a matter of justice or kindness, but part of a frenzied mission to right wrongs – including those wrongs that had been done to her – with violence, if necessary.

Just as she forced charity on the rich, later extracting money from companies by extortion and intimidation, so she imposed luxury on the poor. 'I want my people to get used to walking on deep-pile carpets,' she said. The women's hostel on the Avenida de Mayo was furnished with chandeliers, Dresden figurines and Louis XV chairs. The bed linen was hand-embroidered and the finest materials were used throughout. Thus the rich and poor were bound together in a ritual enactment of Evita's desire to see the one suffer and the other profit.

Of course it was heresy to say such things to a Peronist.

The oriental domes and gothic turrets of the Children's Republic made a rare promise of fantasy in the midst of the dusty pampa. This miniature city, built by the Eva Perón Foundation on land confiscated from wealthy ranchers, was regularly claimed as the inspiration for Disneyland. The child-sized houses, made to a ten-year-old's scale and decorated in marshmallow colours, mimicked styles of architecture from all over the world. The Taj Mahal was here and the Palazzo Ducale, there was a Tudor house and a Scottish castle.

Evita's mini-republic, a cherished project she never saw completed, was intended to entertain children while teaching them to be good Peronists. Covering 120 acres, and including an artificial lake, a farm and a railway, the republic boasted a miniature Supreme Court, Legislature, Chamber of Deputies and fire station. The tiny ministers' offices, containing child-sized desks with scaled-down typewriters and little stacks of forms, were so realistic that the only things missing were a queue of miniature complainants and the inevitable cigarette smoke.

Up to 450 children could be accommodated in the dormitories. For many of them, poor children from the interior, this was their first experience of a holiday away from home. They were well fed here, and sent away with toys and clothes, not second hand, but bought from the best shops in Buenos Aires. Extra tuition was available for those who had fallen behind at school.

Nowadays, although schoolchildren still came here to hold debates in the Chamber of Deputies and to learn about money in the miniature bank, the republic was sadly forsaken. Actually, as a reflection of the country at large, it came painfully close to the truth. The miniature train ran only sporadically, the miniature farm, poorly provided with scraggy sheep and goats, was far from its heyday. Masses were no longer held in the miniature church. It looked as if there had been a miniature coup here, or a miniature revolution.

'Over the years things have been stolen or broken, and they never get replaced,' said a cleaning lady who was mopping the floor in the Supreme Court. 'It's a tragedy how the place has been let go. There used to be three hundred of us working here, now there are only thirty, and who knows how long our jobs will be safe? In this political climate, you can't be sure of anything any more.'

So there was a miniature unemployment problem, too. Yet in one important respect the Children's Republic deviated from the nation it was meant to emulate. Miraculously, Evita's authority had survived here. The main avenue was still named after her, as avenues, hospitals, streets and towns had once been all over Argentina. In a square at one end of the city there was still a golden bust of her, and it must have been one of the only surviving monuments to her in the country – I had certainly never seen another. The inscription commemorated Evita's efforts in securing the vote for women, in 1947.

Leaning on her mop in the Supreme Court, the cleaning lady waxed nostalgic; she told me how Evita once came to share barbecues with the workers on Saturdays. At night, she said, *la Señora* would sometimes arrive unannounced and walk through the silent dormitories, checking that all was well with the sleeping children. It was a poignant image. Was she, in some way, trying to settle the debt of her own unhappy childhood?

Did she see herself as an angel of mercy? School books – which were heavily politicised – encouraged children to regard Evita as an envoy of God who, having decided 'to put an end to so much iniquity, sent his favourite angel to earth . . . and one day God, seeing that she had carried out his wish, ordered her return'.

I wandered around Buenos Aires and, while wandering, I looked for Evita. The iconic version was not hard to find. Hanging from newspaper stands with Elvis and Madonna, she wore the tender, airbrushed smile that was most popular with her fans. She was often to be seen on magazine covers and billboards and on television programmes that sought to untangle the many mysteries of her life.

So much for the legend, but what memory did the streets retain of the teenager who had arrived in Buenos Aires bent on fame and money? I looked for one or two of the cafés she had frequented, closed now. I sat with Bolivian maids and their boyfriends, in the Plaza del Congreso, near to the boarding house where Evita might have spent her first weeks in the capital. 'I imagined', she wrote, 'that large cities were marvellous places where only wealth existed; and everything I heard about them from other people confirmed this belief. They talked about the great city as if it were a wonderful paradise where everything was beautiful and outstanding and I seemed to feel, from what they said, that the people were more *real* than those I saw around me in my town.'

But, far from a paradise, Evita had found the big city hard and humiliating. The ill-treatment of theatre directors and lovers hardened her, the shame of her illegitimacy impressed itself on her heart. She was 'continuously intimidated' by the poverty and unhappiness she saw around her. Was that when Evita started to burn, or was it even earlier? There were neighbours from her home town who remembered her as a child of mystifying fury. 'From every period of my life,' Evita wrote in 'My Life's Cause', 'I retain the memory of some injustice tormenting me and tearing me apart.'

Passing the Ministry of Labour one day, I asked a policewoman if it was possible to see Evita's old office, expecting that it was not – at least not without some considerable form-filling. But the policewoman was not sure; apparently this was an unusual request and she went away to ask someone more senior. When she returned, to my amazement she led me to the elegant wood-panelled room and left me there alone. Minimally furnished, the office was dominated by Evita's desk, the very heart of the Peronist revolution, where she had sat, for hours on end, receiving her *descamisados*, the poor, sick and dispossessed. It was her 'humble imitation of Christ': the poor had only to ask and they would receive unconditionally. She would give them everything she had not had.

Was it thousands or millions who had passed through this office? The statistics, alone, of Evita's life easily overwhelmed rational thought. There were the half a million sewing machines, 400,000 pairs of shoes, 200,000 cooking pots given away by the Foundation in one year. In 1951, Evita was matron of honour at a wedding for 1,608 couples. When she fell ill, thousands gathered outside her residence to pray for the salvation of the 'Spiritual Leader of the Nation'. In her honour, workers vied to break the record for continuous labour, pilgrims walked across the country on broken legs. At least one person fasted to death and there were suicides, because people thought that Evita's death might cause the end of the world. In fact, the night she died was a sort of apocalypse in Buenos Aires. Dozens of people were killed in the panic and more than 2,000 were treated for injuries. Half a million kissed her body, as it lay in state. Forty thousand wrote to the Vatican petitioning her canonisation.

I stood for a time in the room, wondering what to do with this historic moment. I tried to imagine Evita at the desk, and the hordes of people who had filled this room daily with their woes. But apart from a blotter and an ink-well, which might have been Evita's, there were no clues here, no greater haunting than one might find in any other corner of the city. The ghosts had gone from this place, though they still lingered on the street corners, the shanty towns, the plaza, the cemeteries of Buenos Aires.

Now there was talk that a Hollywood film might be made, based on the rock opera *Evita* by Andrew Lloyd Webber and Tim Rice, and the capital buzzed with indignation. Hollywood's bid provoked a rash of possessive graffiti: 'Evita is sacred,' 'Evita belongs to the workers.'

'They've got a damn nerve!' shouted our host at a supper-party in one of the suburbs. He slammed a fist on the table. 'Let them criticise anyone, even Perón, but not my Evita. The woman was a saint!'

'I think there could be bombs, or worse, if they try to make a film,' said María Luisa. 'Why not? It's happened before.'

With the exception of those who had spent their political exile in Europe, many Argentines believed *Evita* to be a sincere musical tribute to the woman they still thought of as First Lady. President Menem, who had been imprisoned, but never exiled, had therefore warmly offered the American film-director Oliver Stone full access to government buildings, including the hallowed presidential balcony overlooking the Plaza de Mayo. It was only when government aides explained how the musical impugned Evita's moral integrity that an appalled Dr Menem abruptly withdrew his invitation, declaring the musical 'a total and absolute infamy'.

Peronists were relieved that Hollywood had been thwarted, but there was still a concern that the film might simply be made elsewhere, and the original insult allowed to stand uncontested. People began to talk of the need for an Argentine film. A spate of television programmes revisited the controversial terrain of Peronism, and Evita returned as a vivid topic of conversation to the nation's dinner-tables, prompting rows and table-thumping the length and breadth of the country.

Many Argentines claimed not to be opposed to a film being made, so long as the truth were told. But whose truth? As usual, truth was a matter of affiliation. Love or hatred for Evita was handed down in families. She was a saint or a whore, there could be no middle way. Even decades after Perón, families in Buenos Aires still defined themselves as 'peronista' or 'anti-peronista'. 'My whole family hates Evita,' said Martín, the fashion journalist, whose aunt had been threatened with a branding iron when she refused to worship at an altar honouring Evita.

When hatred and infatuation ran so deep, could there ever be an objective appraisal of Evita's life? Historian Felix Luna believed such a thing was almost impossible. 'She put herself beyond the critics' reach by turning herself into a myth before she died,' he said.

Although she had died only forty years previously – and many of her contemporaries were still alive – the facts of Evita's life were hard to ascertain. Had she arrived in Buenos Aires at fifteen, with her mother, or with a tango singer, or had she been older and arrived alone? No one knew for sure. Was she small and stocky or willowy, luminously beautiful or plain? Early acquaintances could not agree. The burning woman General Perón remembered meeting had long blonde hair spilling over her shoulders, but the photographs clearly showed that she was still a brunette then. As for her chastity, there was evidence of one or two miserable experiences on the casting couch and someone said that Evita had lived six months with a man, before meeting Perón; then again, a fellow actor claimed she was 'innocence personified'. It ought to have been possible to extract malice and idolatry from the equation and be left with something like the truth, but Evita's truth had been so vitiated. The combined efforts of her admirers and her enemies had ensured that, just as she would have no end, nor would her beginnings ever be certain.

Evita did more than anyone to muddy the waters. Before she married Perón, she saw to it that many documents and photographs relating to her early life, including her birth certificate, were destroyed or disappeared. On their wedding certificate, her place of birth was changed and the date of it advanced, probably in an attempt to disguise her illegitimacy. Argentina's new First Lady created a history and an identity to serve her purposes, and her invention was so successful that three men later dared to claim this iconic creation as their own. The first was Evita's hairdresser, who devised her elegant chignon and taught her how to dress. The second, Perón himself, told an interviewer, 'Eva Perón was a product of mine.'

The third had arguably the best claim. Dr Pedro Ara, the prestigious Spanish embalmer who could work miracles with dead flesh, had indeed created a posthumous version of Evita. At a cost of one hundred thousand dollars, he laboured on her body for a year, replacing her life's fluids with a mixture of glycerine and formaldehyde and coating her body with a thin layer of plastic. People who saw the finished result sometimes fell to their knees, as if in the presence of a miracle. Perón wondered momentarily if his wife had come back to life. Dr Ara had made Evita immortal.

Who was Evita, *really*? Perhaps the details of a life that is over need not matter, unless they become articles of faith, with the destiny of other people dependent on them. It so happened that two basic tenets of Peronism depended on controversial episodes of Evita's life. The first concerned her part in Perón's rise to power.

By 1944, Perón was minister for war, labour and social security and by far the most commanding member of the military dictatorship led by General Farrell. Charismatic, handsome and determined, he spoke for a class of people who had never before been addressed by Argentine politics – the massive number of immigrant workers who laboured without benefits or rights. Perón encouraged the broadening of unions, introduced compulsory arbitration, a minimum wage, paid holidays, medical care and retirement pay. These dramatic reforms won him an army of followers that would be loyal to the general until he died. However, the power that Perón was amassing, and the flaunting of Evita as a mistress he seemed in no hurry to marry, incensed the more conservative element in the military government. After an incident in which a friend of Evita's was given a prominent post in government, a group of officers demanded he resign. Perón did so, but not without making a 'farewell' speech to thousands which was calculated to infuriate the government. The next day he was arrested.

It was during Perón's incarceration that the remarkable 17 October revolution took place, with a million workers converging on the Plaza de Mayo, demanding their leader's release. The mass demonstration was, remarkably, peaceful. 'It was the mob we had always feared so much,' wrote Delfina Bunge de Gálvez, 'yet when we looked out we were amazed … because the mob before our eyes seemed as if touched by a miraculous transformation. These visitors were gay and calm. There were none of the hostile faces or raised fists of previous years.'

Powerless to contain the masses, since many of the police had joined with them, the government collapsed in the face of Perón's supporters, and four months later he was president.

Peronist doctrine held that this victory was, in part, Evita's. There were stories of Evita seen here and there, consulting with trade unionists, organising meetings and running through the streets, stoking up resistance – her heroism could be toned up or down, depending on the degree of your Peronism. But the stories contradicted one another and, yet again, the truth slipped away. There was no evidence that Evita had led the events leading to Perón's victory, and the more objective historians dismissed it.

Evita's other great act of heroism, in Peronist eyes, was her historic renunciation of the candidacy to vice-president in June 1951. After months of speculation that Evita would stand as Perón's deputy in the election of 1952, the General Workers' Congress called a rally at which she was expected publicly to accept the people's mandate. Again, there was a huge turnout, and free coaches were arranged to bring people to the capital from the provinces, with cinema tickets and refreshments included in the package.

Yet when the historic question was put to Evita – would she stand for vice-president? – she would not commit herself, asking for a few days to think over her decision. This was unexpected: why had such an event been organised, if not to frame the historic moment of Evita's acceptance? The crowd pressed her for an answer and Evita wavered: she would not give one. I had watched the film and seen how Evita quietly surveyed the enormous crowd. There were dozens of theories as to what held her back – by then she already knew that she was terminally ill, it was rumoured that the army did not want her candidacy, that Perón himself did not want it. Whatever the reason, for those few minutes of wavering, Evita had the country in the palm of her hand. She must have gauged, then, the extraordinary scope of her power. For all that her speeches relentlessly praised Perón and denigrated herself, she must have known that she was the strong one. Without her, Peronism was sure to founder.

There were two necropolises in Buenos Aires, two mini-cities that were not intended for the entertainment of children. In these miniature republics, the labyrinthine streets were lined with mausoleums, chapels and temples. Alabaster angels wept and prayed. All the occupants of the little houses were dead.

Death appealed to Argentine snobbery. It was expensive and classy to display your loved one's mahogany coffin in a family shrine that had glass doors – an artful invitation to voyeurs. A sunny afternoon in Buenos Aires might cheerfully be spent strolling around one necropolis or the other, peering through the lace-curtained windows at the coffins and at the family photographs which adorned the marble altars. Perón's tomb was in the middle-class Chacarita cemetery, among actors and writers, dentists and accountants, on the outskirts of the city. Evita, in a final triumph of social-climbing, had entered Recoleta, the dominion of the Oligarchy. The necropolis at Recoleta represented Buenos Aires society after death, with its snobbery, its hierarchy and its ambition intact. Here lay the country's founding fathers, the dictators and the philosophers, the high-society families. The statues were made by the best European artists.

Three people were gathered in the confined space outside Evita's family tomb. One was a strange youth with sallow skin. He wore a thick, black mourning suit and an armband on which a childish hand had printed 'Evita' in letters that sloped backwards. The boy stuck a dozen roses, one by one, through the grille of the door to her tomb. He rested a hand on the brass plaque bearing Evita's name, wincing slightly, as if this were an electric connection, then he started to pray. His lips, immodestly plump, moved quickly through his prayers, accumulating moisture as they went. Then the boy put his mouth to the brass plaque he had been touching and brushed his swollen lips over each letter of her name. It was a strangely repugnant sight.

The other two were American tourists and they were wearing shorts, although it was not hot. Slung about with cameras, both these men had great sturdy legs which were speckled brown and covered in hairy curlicues. The watermark tans on their thighs proclaimed many months' determined sight-seeing.

This group of three seemed to present an allegory: here was the child of dictatorships, small and sickly, oppressed by his black suit and his religion. And here were his North American cousins, enjoying the freedom to be well fed and badly dressed. They did not pray, but they took photographs.

'I would love to see the bawdy,' said the fatter of them, scratching a curlicued thigh. He clucked with frustration, as if a glimpse of the dead Evita ought to have been part of the deal; his South American experience would be incomplete without it. The black-button eyes bored into the locked door of the shrine. The legs hesitated, as if there might be some way round this impediment.

'Perhaps they keep the real bawdy someplace else,' said his companion.

There were many rumours about what had happened to Evita's body after the 1955 coup which promised to eradicate the cult of the Peróns. The incoming government had set out to prove that the plastic doll they found on the fifth floor of the Workers' Congress was a dummy, a hoax. When tests confirmed that it really was Evita, they were terrified. How could Peronism properly be extirpated from the country, when the movement's greatest symbol was still present and, apparently, non-biodegradable? Evita must be got rid of, but a normal burial was out of the question because of the danger of creating a shrine. The Catholic dictators were wary of cremation. So it was that Colonel Moori Koenig was entrusted with the body, and given instructions to find a secret burial place for it. That was how Evita's body turned up hidden in the attic of an office block near our flat.

Something happened to Moori Koenig. He must have gone mad, people said, for he fell in love with the body and could not part with it. It was alleged that he had committed 'unChristian acts' with it. The body had to be taken from him and finally the junta decided that it was not safe to have it in Argentina. Evita was sent to be buried in Rome, under the guise of an Italian housewife, while replica bodies were apparently sent as decoys to other countries. President Aramburu ordered that the details of the burial be enclosed in an envelope and given to his lawyer which, in the event of his death, would be passed to the next president of Argentina. Thus he saved himself the burden of knowing where Evita had finally come to rest, but, if Aramburu had known, he might have been able to save his own life from the Montonero interrogators.

Evita's posthumous peregrination was to enter Peronist mythology as the great injustice, the unforgivable humiliation. When the body was returned, after its eighteen-year exile, rumours about its state ran riot. Some people claimed Evita had been horribly violated, raped and urinated on, cigarettes stubbed out on her. Others said that this was not the real body at all.

I once met a woman who worshipped Evita. She had a painting depicting Evita as a saint, a troubling vision in lipstick and a halo. And this woman really *had* seen Evita's body. She had accompanied Evita's sister Blanca to inspect the body in 1974, when the corpse first arrived back in Buenos Aires. 'She'd taken quite a battering during her travels,' the woman told me. 'Her nose was broken and she was generally in bad shape, apart from her hair, which was beautiful. But don't worry, she's been totally recycled now. She'll last for a hundred years.'

The two brass plaques affixed to the wall of her tomb represented the Evita who loved:

> Don't cry for me, I am neither far away nor lost
> but an essential part of your existence,
> all the love and the pain were foreseen.
> I carried out a humble imitation of Christ,
> let it be an example
> to those who follow me

and the Evita who burned:

> I have an uncontrollable desire to burn up my life
> if by burning it I can shed light on the way and the happiness of the
> Argentine people
> I shall return and be millions!

Given the evolution of her fury, it was hardly surprising that Evita's last dictum, written on her death-bed, was more violent than anything she had previously produced. 'My Message' disappeared before it could be published and may have been stolen during the ransacking of the presidential residence in 1955. Nearly forty years later the document popped up, unannounced and unexplained, at a furniture auction. Now, decades after she had written it, when it could finally be guaranteed to fall on deaf ears, Evita's message had been delivered.

Our newsagent rolled his eyes when I bought my copy. 'What's the point', he said, 'after all these years?'

I read the short book in a café, with the feeling that I was reading pornography, the words were so hot, so brutal. In 'My Message', Evita exhorted her followers to take up arms against the ruling class, the army and the church, to brand the faces of traitors with hot irons. 'I don't understand half-measures or balanced arguments,' she wrote. 'I only recognise two words, which I hold like cherished daughters in my heart: hatred and love.'

Few bookshops in Buenos Aires chose to stock 'My Message'. The fury and hatred expressed in the book were no longer in tune with the way Evita's fans wanted to remember her. The warmongering Evita had retreated in Argentina's collective psyche to be replaced by something much safer.

Hugo Palavecino, a grave-tender, was looking over the cemetery wall the day they secretly laid Evita to rest. Now he was the only person, apart from her sisters, permitted to enter the family mausoleum. Evita, who once had dressmakers, hairdressers, make-up artists, had only Hugo to attend to her now.

'She's about five metres under where we're standing now,' said Hugo, squinting in the sunshine. 'Her coffin's secured behind steel plates, to protect her from assaults. The vault's proof against burglars, bombs, even a nuclear attack.'

All that steel and earth to protect Evita from Argentina's rage. And to protect Argentina from hers, too, for there was no *bronca* to rival Evita's.

I shall return and be millions! It was Evita's most famous saying, although, like so much else, it was apocryphal. And yet, twenty years after her death, Evita had indeed returned to wreak a bloody revenge on Argentina. It was precisely her message of fanaticism, of mixed passions, that inspired the guerilla uprising of the 1970s. The Montoneros, who came to believe that Evita was a greater Peronist even than Perón himself, based their philosophy explicitly on her exhortation 'to burn with the sacred fire of fanaticism'.

Was Argentina's *bronca* connected to Evita? Felix Luna had lamented as much to me. 'Evita's work in the field of welfare was extraordinary,' he said. 'She was a remarkable woman who touched people very directly. But she sowed a seed of aggression in Argentine society. I hope we never see the likes of her again.'

I asked Hugo what he thought about when he was five metres below ground, alone with one of history's most famous women. 'I try not to think about it at all,' he said. 'Peronism was a time of great tyranny and Argentina should put all that hatred and violence in the past. If I think anything, I suppose I hope that she's finally at rest.'

After Evita died, altars glorifying her sprang up in homes everywhere. Children learned to pray 'Our Mother who art in heaven'. The thousands of Argentines who had written to their idol were instructed to keep writing to her as if she had never left them. Sometimes they received a letter back, signed by Evita and promising, 'I am happy here with the angels.'

Argentina's new National Library stood as a testament to the belief that truth can be erased. A brutalist building, it squatted on vast concrete haunches, like a defecating monster, over the spot where the Peróns' presidential palace used to be. The palace was ransacked and razed after the 1955 coup, two years after the death of Eva Perón, in a concerted attempt to banish all record of the Peróns from the national memory. Under the new government, it became illegal to mention the Peróns, to own photographs of them or even to use acronyms such as 'PV', *Perón Vuelve* (Perón will return). The hundreds of statues of Evita smiling across the country were destroyed. The cities that had adopted her name changed back.

The library had taken more than twenty-five years to build and, when I visited, it was an empty universe. Dozens of freshly minted bureaucrats were already in place, waiting with rubber-stamps and cultivating their *bronca* – but nobody knew how many months it might be before the books themselves arrived. A vigorous young woman was in charge of guided tours around the library. My group included an elderly man carrying a collection of P. G. Wodehouse in English. When I was introduced to the others as British, he said, 'Good afternoon,' in English with a formal nod and a little click of the heels.

Our guide took us on an exhausting journey around the library, opening an endless succession of doors on to one large empty room after another. 'This is the exhibition room,' she said, indicating one empty room, 'and here is the reading room,' showing us another. 'We shall have the newest computers and link-ups to libraries all over the world. Later there will be a theatre for lectures.' The Wodehouse man appeared silently at my side. 'Top hole,' he murmured specifically for my benefit. 'How spiffing.'

Downstairs, the guide told us that the benches in the public areas had been designed to feel uncomfortable after two minutes. 'We don't want to encourage people to hang around.' I tried one of the benches and found that it was indeed very uncomfortable, the concave wooden surfaces jutting into shoulders and thighs.

A library without books, chairs designed for discomfort, such paradoxes would have delighted Jorge Luis Borges, himself once director of the National Library, though famously 'promoted' by Perón to inspector of poultry. Borges had loathed the Peróns and he followed the unimaginative upper-class insult of calling Evita a whore. A poem containing the name Perón, he once said, would fall apart.

One of the longest-serving members of staff told me how Borges used to go down to the store rooms, and wander up and down between the stacks of books, in the dark. 'He was already blind by then, but he loved to be alone with the books. We could hear his stick tapping as he went along.' It was the right way to remember Borges, an old man alone in a darkness crowded by books. Borges imagined the universe to be an 'infinite library'.

Hovering high above the acres of bookless space, on the fourth floor, the director Enrique Pavón Pereyra was a crumpled figure with an expression of boundless sorrow that seemed appropriate to his empty surroundings. His big old face supported a cloud of white hair. I had been warned that he would know nothing about the library. 'It's just a political appointment,' one of the employees explained. He had got his job because he was a prominent Peronist, indeed he was the author of Perón's authorised biography. But the interview was already arranged and so I took a lift through the space to his office, which was guarded by two cruel-looking young women with red fingernails.

Inside Señor Pavón Pereyra was swinging idly on an office chair behind a vast, empty desk. A flag stood beside the desk and there were framed photographs of the library's three most famous directors, Borges, Lugones and Groussac, all of them blind. There were also photographs of President Menem and of General Perón.

The director gestured towards the latter. 'A dear old friend,' he said. 'I've written a book about him, you know. You should read it.'

We sat down on opposite sides of the desk. I asked Señor Pavón Pereyra how many books were in the library's collection. The director swung thoughtfully on his chair, but he was not thinking about my question. His mind was decades back.

'She died just below where we're sitting, you know.' He waved a hand at the newly carpeted floor.

'Evita?'

'Yes, Evita.' He looked curiously at me. 'Where are you from, young girl?'

From Britain, I said. I asked another question about the library. The director, far away, ignored it.

Suddenly, shockingly, his eyes filled with tears.

'Why do you no longer love us?' he asked.

'Love you? Who?'

'England! Like a beautiful woman who spurns her lover, England has turned her back on Argentina. How can we forget that love and that desertion?'

Tears rolled down his cheeks. 'A faithful suitor keeps hoping to be heard, you know, but finally he abandons hope. He *will* abandon hope.'

'I'm sure we do still love you,' I said, awkwardly aware that it was the first time I had ever had to say such a thing in an interview. I felt like a minor actress unexpectedly handed a romantic lead.

'Our countries used to be so close. It was very important to us, that cultural link.' He looked sharply up. 'You used to send money. We could do with some money to buy more books.'

'But we don't have enough money now even for British libraries. We aren't such a rich country any more.' I felt I was faltering.

Señor Pavón Pereyra leaned urgently across the empty wastes of his desk. 'You must go back to England and tell her to love us again. There must still be some chance – why else would they have written that beautiful musical?'

Had Señor Pavón Pereyra seen *Evita*?

No, he had not, but, like most Argentines, he still thought that it was a wonderful homage. 'Don't Cry for Me Argentina' was regularly played in shopping malls and to soothe the checkout queues in Hawaii and Disco.

My questions about the library were obviously redundant, so I resigned myself to leaving. 'Wait a minute, dear,' Señor Pavón Pereyra said. 'Take this.' He delved into one of the drawers of his enormous desk and retrieved a photograph of himself, looking exactly as he looked now, with the same cloud of hair and a face ready for tears. I stood up to leave and he embraced me fondly. 'Come back whenever you want, dear,' he said. 'Treat this as your home.' I walked out, past the cruel-looking girls, and felt the stirrings of a great compassion.

CHAPTER SEVEN

Las Malvinas Son Argentinas

A GIANT MAP OF the world occupied one wall in the office of the foreign minister, Guido di Tella. It was a British map, but with an important amendment made to the group of islands off Argentina's Atlantic coast. With minute care, the words 'Falkland Islands' and the brackets which usually encased 'Islas Malvinas' had been concealed under blue tape that exactly matched the colour of the surrounding sea. It was a job so skilful that the join could be noticed only by the meandering eye of a peculiarly inattentive journalist. In press conferences, when I should have been applying myself to questions of fishing rights and sovereignty, I dreamed instead of the official who had been charged with finding the precise shade of tape necessary to this tiny alteration of the truth. I saw him darting in and out of stationery shops, sweating in his suit, concerned for his promotion prospects. Or had the minister himself undertaken this mission?

Sovereignty of the Falklands was not a burning issue in Argentina, but a simple matter of right and wrong. Everybody in the country knew – by force of repetition, if for no other reason – that the Malvinas rightly belonged to Argentina. 'Las Malvinas son Argentinas' was a slogan repeated in school-rooms up and down the country, printed on the back of notebooks and rulers, on T-shirts, badges and mugs. It was emblazoned on the tired bunting which was meant to adorn the Avenida de Mayo on national holidays, but which effectively hung there for most of the year. Old men sat at stalls on street corners, selling Malvinas souvenirs, alongside badges of Evita and plastic Argentine flags.

Although the islands were not theirs, the Argentines treated them as such with admirable determination, including them in national weather reports and honouring them in street names and businesses. When the economy stabilised sufficiently to allow the issue of stamps, the first set laid claim to the Malvinas. Every year Dr Menem opened Congress with an emotional vow to regain this 'stolen' territory. 'Even now I can visualise the Argentine flag fluttering over our islands!' the president cried, to rapturous applause and cheers. He never lost an opportunity to promise that the islands would be returned to Argentina by the year 2000.

'Can you imagine if he does get them back?' asked my friend Guillermo. 'He'll be president for ever.'

'We just wish he would stop saying it,' a British Embassy official confided.

Some way along the road that led from Ezeiza Airport to the city of Buenos Aires, there was a large sign that seemed, from a distance, to offer advice about traffic control or the proximity of service stations. Actually it had nothing to do with either; it did not exist to welcome visitors to Buenos Aires, nor to advise them of twinnings with metropolises around the world. The sign was simply there to warn visitors of the extent of the nation's obsession. It read, 'Las Malvinas son Argentinas,' and the insinuation seemed to be, 'If you don't accept this, then don't come any further.' *Las Malvinas Son Argentinas*: easy to sing, easy to chant, it was as natural a slogan as 'Beanz Meanz Heinz'. To suggest anything else sounded oddly ungrammatical. When I started a question, 'If the Malvinas *were* Argentine', I felt as if I had hypothesised on the blueness of the sky.

People entered my life on the nod, like tango partners and after a few jaunty manoeuvres – a flirtation on a street corner, a row on a crossed line – they were gone again. Most days I had brief encounters with strangers in the city. There was so many queues to wait in and so many grievances to be aired in them. One young woman I met in a waiting room confided that she was giving up a life-long analysis habit to become a clown. 'Being a clown is a better therapy,' she said, 'because it forces you to do something positive with your sadness.' Waiting for books at the library I met a Serbian refugee who was contemptuous of Argentine fashion. 'I must have been the last person to buy leggings in Belgrade, but I was the first in Buenos Aires.'

When people found out that I was British, they often wanted to ask me about the Falklands. 'When are you giving us back the Malvinas?' was a fairly usual question. Usually I laughed and said that Argentina was welcome to the islands as far as I was concerned. But once, in a queue to pay the electricity bill, bad humour made me snap: 'Why do you want them?'

My questioner, a whiskery man in his sixties, was momentarily baffled by this response: his thoughts about the islands had never been stretched beyond the slogan. He paused for thought. Why should he want them? There was not yet any suggestion of oil being found on the islands – though, to be fair, when the question of oil did arise it little affected Argentine passions. The national attachment to the islands was fundamentally sentimental.

'Because they're ours,' he protested finally. He reached for the familiar words taught at school. 'They were unjustly usurped by English pirates.' The man managed to convey both the original injustice and the unreasonableness of the English pirate presently before him with a shrugged spreading of his hands.

'But the Dutch discovered them first,' I said. 'And the British landed there before Spain.'

The man blinked and goggled. His whiskers twitched nervously. This information was not included on the notebooks and rulers.

'Besides, there are two thousand people living there who want to be British, not Argentine,' I pressed on. 'What are you going to do about them?'

'Por Dios, mujer,' sighed the man.

Noticing that her compatriot was flagging, a woman in the queue behind the whiskery man took up the baton. 'You can't go around taking other people's land,' she said sharply, as though admonishing a child. 'They're ours and you ought to give them back.'

She started to fan herself indignantly with her electricity bill, this burst of patriotic anger having warmed her blood. The room was hot and ill-lit, and the glum shuffling of men and women in half a dozen queues seemed to slow the circulation of air. Somewhere in the distance I could hear the familiar music of two-fingered typing. We were all being punished in this slow-moving room, because this was the centre you came to when you had already missed two opportunities to pay a bill. Argentine bills were remarkably complex documents with many different figures in different boxes and various addresses at which payment would be expected, depending on the date you went to pay. It was not unusual to queue for an hour at one place, only to be told that you should have been queuing somewhere else on the other side of the city. The process could take hours, and so people tended to put it off, which only made matters worse.

The waiting had made my legs and head ache and now I felt unreasonably irritated by the whiskery man's sour breath, billowing over my shoulder. Why, in this airless room, did everyone insist on standing so close to one another? If I turned and poked him in the chest I could take out the whole queue, like skittles. I felt *bronca* unfurling in my chest. Perhaps it was mean of me to argue about the Falklands when the islands meant so much to Argentina and so little to Britain, I thought, but they ought to apply a better logic to their argument. I turned back to face the woman who had admonished me.

'Everyone took everyone else's land a hundred and fifty years ago,' I said. 'Didn't Spain take Argentina from the Indians? Didn't you try to take bits of Chile? It was the way of the world.'

The woman flapped her bill and shook her head vigorously, creating a fluster of disapproval.

'It's not the same . . .' grumbled the whiskery man.

'Well, would you go and live there, if you got them back?'

Now they looked at me as if I were a disconcerting new addition to the zoo, a lizard slipping off crinkled skin, or a baboon turning to reveal a shockingly pink anus. People further back in the queue were also beginning to regard me with suspicion. Fortunately, my number was called: it was time to pay up.

'The truth is that, if we got the islands back tomorrow, we'd have to send two thousand civil servants to live there, because no one else would want to go,' Congressman Juan Canals told me. There was also a map of the world in his office, but since it was Argentine no modification had been needed. 'Why should people want to go and live on a windswept island in the middle of the Atlantic, when they don't even want to go and live in Patagonia?'

Señor Canals sat on a governmental commission which was examining possible solutions to the Falklands stalemate. Though Britain refused to discuss sovereignty – that was one of the terms of the resumption of diplomatic links in 1990 – Argentina was still pressing its case at the United Nations, where it received sympathetic hearings. Currently the government was studying the case of the Aland Islands, which belonged to Finland, though the inhabitants were Swedish. The foreign minister had visited Aland, and was enthusiastic about implementing a similar scheme on the Falklands. The 2,000 islanders could keep their British passports, their customs and education, he promised. Life on the islands need not change. Listening to his assurances, it seemed as if Argentine pride really would be satisfied simply by the spectacle of the national flag fluttering over the islands, as in the president's tearful evocation.

On one occasion, I asked the minister why Argentina should maintain an island populated by hostile Britons. 'In my case I would appreciate the existence, in part of our territory, of people with a different language, culture and tradition,' he told me. 'It would help us to form a more tolerant view of the world. That might be the islands' most important contribution to our culture.'

It was a touching image, except that the islanders – nicknamed kelpers after a local species of seaweed – were not at all keen to make such a generous contribution. Indeed, it was unfathomable to most Argentines what these people did want. They imagined the kelpers as belligerent farmers who spent their days drinking tea and singing homilies to the Queen. They thought it odd that Britain insisted on bowing to the demands of such peculiar people.

'We are resigned to the fact that the British will never accept anything without the consent of the islanders,' said Señor Di Tella, 'and the kelpers are uncertain about our intentions because we have not been a democracy for long. So the only weapon we have is our capacity to convince. Things will change in time.'

The foreign minister struck me as a man of somewhat divided loyalties. His president had charged him with returning the Falklands to Argentine sovereignty by the year 2000, and he longed to secure this victory – it would surely be regarded as the greatest triumph in the nation's history. At the same time he was an Anglophile who wore tweeds and had taught at Oxford during his political exile. He had been reprimanded by the president when he refused to qualify Britain's sinking of the Argentine ship the *General Belgrano* as a 'war crime'. 'Nobody can question the right to sink an enemy boat, when at war,' he had reasoned, before retraction and an apology were forced on him.

How could Argentina possibly endear itself to the hostile kelpers by the year 2000? The foreign minister had launched what he called a 'charm offensive'. He wrote to the islanders at Christmas and on the Queen's birthday; one Christmas he sent 480 families a comic BBC cartoon about penguins and boasted that only eight videos had been returned to him, though it was said that others had been tossed on to minefields left by the Argentines on the islands. Señor Di Tella's charm was regarded with profound suspicion by the islanders, who referred to him as 'Mr Smoothie', but still he pressed on. He had given the islanders his telephone number and invited them to call him any time. Though some had rung up to blow raspberries, evidently others had been more positive. 'It's something that I have to be very discreet about,' Señor Di Tella said.

Press conferences at the Foreign Ministry could sometimes feel like seminars in philosophy or semantics, as Señor Di Tella struggled to convey the unique importance of the islands to Argentine sentiment. The crux of the matter was that Britain and Argentina had different approaches to 'nationhood' and territory, he explained. 'Fatherland is a threatening word for you, a word with negative associations. But for us *patria* is the homeland.' National identity in Argentina, he said, was profoundly allied to land. It was intolerable for Argentines to know that their homeland was mutilated, as they felt it had been by the British.

'The Malvinas are a very powerful symbol, crucial to national identity in this country,' said Osvaldo, one of the three men who ran the newspaper stall outside our front door. 'You have to imagine that you have a country where fifty per cent of the population are immigrants. How are you going to unite them under one flag? Since the early days of the republic, the Malvinas have been deliberately used as a common cause to make people feel Argentine. All school-children have it bored into them that the Malvinas were stolen by British in 1833. It's the only thing the whole country can agree on.'

Osvaldo could speak with some authority on the Falklands, since he had lost his job as a history teacher for suggesting that the invasion was wrong. He was softly spoken, philosophical about the loss of a job he had loved. 'I was careless,' he shrugged. 'I didn't realise that the school was full of children from military families.'

It was a wonder to me how the newsagents managed to make a living from their stall, since they often gave us a discount on news-papers and were loath to sell the expensive European fashion maga-zines at all. 'Why pay eight dollars for it, when you can borrow it free?' was one seller's imperfect logic. But it was useful having a historian on the doorstep, and in the course of researching articles, providing the lift was working, I occasionally went down to ask

Osvaldo about something or to get a quote. We often talked about the Falklands, Osvaldo leaning across the piles of newspapers and glossy magazines to an audience which might grow to include several curious passers-by. Sometimes Máximo stopped off on his way back home, to rave about the state of the nation. Osvaldo's balding head and gold-rimmed spectacles made him look erudite and even monkish against the glossy background of *Playboys*, sports magazines and imported *Vogues*.

'By 1981, the economy was going very badly and more and more people were asking questions about the disappeared,' Osvaldo explained to me and whoever else would listen. 'The military government desperately needed a "clean" war to wash away the Dirty War. They considered one with Chile over disputed territory in Patagonia, but it was too risky, whereas the Malvinas looked more straightforward and was guaranteed to win them much more favour in the country. Amazingly, they thought that the British would not retaliate and, even more extraordinarily, they gambled that the United States would back Argentina.'

One morning we were talking about the Falklands, Osvaldo lamenting the invasion as usual, when a dapper man in a raincoat arrived to pick up his daily newspaper. Hearing what we were saying, the man became suddenly, almost magically, irate. His face bloomed into colour. He started to brandish the rolled newspaper at Osvaldo.

'What the hell are you saying? Of course it was right to take the islands – they're ours,' he shouted. 'Those British bastards need teaching a lesson. They think they own the world!'

'I'm British,' I said rather too defiantly.

The man spun round to look at me, then he suddenly became polite again: 'Well, I'm sure you're very nice, Señorita. But the rest of the British are bastards' – and off he strode.

The Federation of War Veterans' headquarters stood in the much depleted neighbourhood of San Telmo, an atmospheric *barrio* of cobbled streets and tango bars. On Sundays there was an antiques market in the main square and old men in pinstriped suits stood on the street corners, warbling about their broken hearts for passers-by who cared to stop and listen, or to dance for a while. Carlos Gardel, the greatest *tanguero* of all, smiled from posters in several shop windows.

San Telmo was in the Southside of Buenos Aires, the oldest part of the city. It had once been a neighbourhood of well-to-do families, but outbreaks of yellow fever and cholera ravaged the population in the 1870s, chasing the wealthy to higher settlements on the north side of the city, away from the docks. The abandoned south was taken over by immigrants and low-lifers. Grand, deserted houses were made to accommodate thirty or more straitened families. Brothels opened on street corners and gangs lurked in alleyways. People lived here by cunning and the knife. The Southside was the birthplace of the tango and some said that Argentina's disaffection was born here too.

The presence of a massive open-air slaughter-ground had contributed greatly to the atmosphere of ill health on the Southside at the end of the nineteenth century. At El Saladero, some three or four miles square, cattle had come to be killed in the traditional, brutal way, their throats slit by the gaucho's knife, their bodies left to rot in the open air: at that time the slaughterers were interested only in hides, not meat. In his classic memoir *Far Away and Long Ago*, W. H. Hudson bore gruesome witness to how 'Buenos Ayres came to be the chief pestilential city of the globe and was obliged to call in engineers from England to do something to save the inhabitants from extinction.' His description of the scene at El Saladero, a chilling masterpiece, revealed the crude nature of the settlers' money lust:

Just where the animal was knocked down and killed, it was stripped of its hide and the carcass cut up, a portion of the flesh and the fat being removed and all the rest left on the ground to be devoured by the pariah dogs, the carrion hawks, and a multitude of screaming black-headed gulls always in attendance. The blood so abundantly shed from day to day, mixing with the dust, had formed a crust half a foot thick all over the open space: let the reader try to imagine the smell of this crust and of tons of offal and flesh and bones lying everywhere in heaps. But no, it cannot be imagined. The most dreadful scenes, the worst in Dante's Inferno, for example, can be visualized by the inner eye; and sounds, too, are conveyed to us in a description so that they can be heard mentally; but it is not so with smells. The reader can only take my word for it that this smell was probably the worst ever known on earth ... It was the smell of carrion, of putrefying flesh, and of that old and ever-newly moistened crust of dust and coagulated blood. It was, or seemed, a curiously substantial and stationary smell; travellers approaching or leaving the capital by the great south road, which skirted the killing grounds, would hold their noses and ride a mile or so at a furious gallop until they got out of the abominable stench.

Perhaps it was a squeamish awareness of that blood-soaked earth that caused some of the buildings in San Telmo to shift uneasily on their foundations, as if seeking to uproot themselves from a ghastly history. Lopsided houses leaned on their neighbours for support, and those that had no neighbours relied on wooden crutches supplied by the municipality. Squatters advertised their presence from the dilapidated balconies with strings of washing that looked like flags of surrender. Poor children with skinny brown legs kicked footballs around in the street and there was a strange preponderance of lame, lolloping dogs in San Telmo.

I arrived at the front door of Veterans' House one hot spring afternoon, and rang the bell with a certain trepidation. Famously belligerent, the veterans were wont to refer to the British as 'lackeys of the Queen'. Scotland Yard detectives visiting Argentina in 1993 to investigate a British soldier's allegations of war crimes committed by his own side in the Falklands, had met with a profound suspicion. Why would any government want to investigate the behaviour of its own army? Smelling a plot, the Argentine veterans had made a promise to be as unhelpful as possible, and largely kept it.

With a jangle of old keys, the door opened and I was led into an interior patio where half a dozen men were sitting in a circle drinking maté. The consumption of this bitter tea was usually a communal event: a gourd of dried, shredded maté leaves was filled with hot water; the first drinker sipped the tea through a metal straw called a *bombilla*. Then the gourd was refilled with hot water and passed on. Sharing a maté was an Argentine ritual, particularly among workers and intellectuals, and in these strained circumstances it struck me almost as an act of patriotism. There was a smouldering defiance implicit in the attitude of this circle of men. Several had taken off their shirts, and the fatter stomachs swelled with a gleaming menace. I felt too clothed, too English, too female, as I tripped by them, smiling nervously.

Upstairs, in a dark room where the kettle was boiling for another round of maté, I was introduced to Walter, a fair man in his thirties. He was slim and handsome and his eyes were an unusually pale blue, as if a habit of weeping were wringing the colour from them.

Walter told me that I was lucky to be speaking to him and not to one of the more antagonistic veterans, because he had nothing against the British. 'I have Mapuche Indian blood and I can be violent, but I'm a man of peace.' The experience of war had led quite a few veterans to become pacifists and ecologists, he said. His own ambition was to work as an ecologist on the Falklands, which he would like to see given over for a nature reserve.

But, remembering the aftermath of the war, Walter's Mapuche blood reasserted itself, and he became taut with emotion. 'Our adolescence was ruined,' he said. 'We came home to find ourselves completely marginalised. We were a symbol of the defeat and we had to pay for the sins of our superiors. No one was outraged about what had happened to us, no one offered psychological support.' The pale blue eyes filled easily with tears. 'I'm sorry, but you see I still feel so much *bronca*.'

Walter had been drafted into military service at eighteen and found himself serving in the Falklands just a few months later. He had been a member of that raggedy troop of boys, badly kitted out, barely able to use a gun, who had shocked the British professionals, and ultimately impressed them too, with their courage. The bad treatment meted out to Argentine soldiers by their superiors was notorious. Food packages sent by parents went missing. Dead boys' belongings were never returned to their families. When the soldiers came home, they found themselves all too readily associated with defeat and, more than ten years later, many of them still struggled to get work. The veterans were a pathetic sight in Buenos Aires, begging in the trains and on buses. 'Even if you don't tell people that you were in the war, they always find out, and then they don't want to know you,' said Walter.

His hands and shoulders gestured futility. 'What can we do? We're in a desperate situation. If you add up all the money that's disappeared in corruption scandals over the last ten years, there would easily be enough for a veterans' pension. But we live in a society where there are no rules or morals. The security of the people is in the hands of a corrupt police force, the government steals from its own people, how can anybody feel safe?'

One of the gleaming-bellied men came into the room then to retrieve the boiling kettle, shooting me a suspicious look before he left. Lately the veterans had been complaining of the 'demalvinasisation' of Argentine society. They wanted the government to be more bullish in its demand for sovereignty.

'You see, the Malvinas isn't just a piece of territory,' Walter went on, 'it's part of our identity. It's the only thing that's going to save us from the corruption that's eating up this country.'

I had heard many sentiments attached to the islands, but not that they had the power to end state corruption, improve society.

'You think that Argentina would be a better place to live if you could get the islands back?' I asked.

'Of course it would,' said Walter, 'it stands to reason. It's the one thing that can save us.'

It was meeting Walter that made me appreciate, finally, how much more significant the Falklands were than a clutch of windy islands. They had come to symbolise everything that Argentina had lost – and that loss was staggering. Perhaps no country had ever promised so much and failed so dramatically. Argentina had begun the century as the sixth richest country in the world. It was forecast to be a land of the future, along with Australia or Canada, but even wealthier than these two, the epitome of opportunity in the New World. By the year 2000, the population had been expected to reach, not thirty-two million, as it currently stood, but nearly twice that. 'To govern is to populate,' the president had proclaimed. The vast, fertile land would be filled and cultivated by a new, confident race. Schoolchildren were taught that theirs was a promised land.

The legend of Argentina's wealth was mesmerising. Here was a country of apparently infinite natural resources. The pampa could claim to offer the most fertile soil anywhere on earth. With the minimum of effort applied, the land yielded miracles. The topsoil was so rich it need never be rotated. Beef reared on the pampa was of the finest quality, yet cattle were so abundant that, in the nineteenth century, they were killed for their hides alone, the gaucho slaughterers hacking off the odd bit of meat for their suppers before allowing the rest to putrefy and sink back into the rich earth. Travellers on the pampa were free to kill a cow, eat what they wanted and leave what remained to the vultures – so long as they did not steal the hide. The waste was spectacular, breathtaking.

It was a country of easy money. The British, quick on the scene where money was to be made, spotted that early, and bound Argentina into a trading agreement that would turn out to be much more advantageous to them than to their Latin American partner. Railways were built to transport the wealth to Buenos Aires, and thence to Britain. The Argentine peso soared higher than the American dollar.

On *estancias* the size of small kingdoms, the Oligarchy built country houses in the style of French palaces and castles. They rose, these extraordinary visions, out of plains that were empty for hundreds of miles around. Yet for half the year the owners left them and travelled to Europe, perhaps taking a cow with them, so that the children need not risk foreign milk. Argentines appeared at the opera in Rome and at the races in England. Their ostentatious presence in Paris prompted the expression 'riche comme un Argentin'. Summaries of their wedding lists and parties appeared in a society magazine that also included, in one issue, a cardboard doll of Edward, Duke of Windsor, complete with cut-out costumes.

Landed Argentines looked abroad for all their needs, and shipped in everything, not just paintings, furniture and wood-panelling, but cars, cattle and whole buildings. The squares of Buenos Aires were provided with European statues. The roads were paved with imported cobblestones.

In the first decades of the twentieth century, visitors to Argentina noticed a swaggering confidence in the natives. Ortega y Gasset wrote that they 'do not content themselves with being one nation among others: they hunger for an overarching destiny, they demand of themselves a proud future. They would not know a history without triumph.'

What went wrong? Something terrible had happened, but no one could put a finger on the exact source of the disaster. The descendants of Spaniards blamed Italian immigration, while the Italians pointed to the original failures of Spanish colonialism. 'We were brought up to believe that we could have everything,' one of Raquel's patients told me. 'Wealth, culture, the Malvinas ... We were conned.'

Argentina's pomposity and arrogance were pure fanfare; at heart, there was a powerful atmosphere of self-hatred in the country. Even Santiago, nine years old, told me gravely, 'The Argentines are mediocre.'

One evening I was taken to supper at the Jockey Club, so potent a symbol of the Oligarchy that Perón had relieved himself of a little class frustration by having the original premises looted and burned. My host was an industrialist and he was accompanied by an eccentric upper-class woman whose underwear outlined itself quite clearly against her skirt. Eccentricity and a relaxed attitude to underwear were rare in Buenos Aires, so I warmed to her. As we ate steak in the dining room, she told me of her ambition to hunt buffalo, though her present, apparently opposite project was to save the guanaco, a sort of llama which was reared for wool then slaughtered, unnecessarily she thought. She was leaving for Patagonia the next morning. 'How long are you going for?' I asked. 'As long as it takes,' she replied. 'I won't come back until I've saved them.'

After coffee we toured those few club rooms that were open to women. My host, respecting the building's history, spoke in a murmur, and I felt it appropriate to murmur back. 'You probably have preconceptions about this place,' he said, 'but, believe me, the people who founded this club belonged to the greatest generation of Argentines. I don't pretend to be descended from them. She is.' He indicated the woman with the assertive underwear, striding ahead of us. My host gripped my elbow, ostensibly for support – he walked with a limp – but it felt like a subtle oppression: he wanted to steer me, to make me agree with him. We entered the drawing room, where large oil paintings evoked English hunting scenes with tangles of dogs falling on foxes. Wild-eyed and slavering, the dogs looked too ferocious to have been painted by an English artist, even if they were killing foxes.

Since he kept extolling the greatness of the country's founding fathers, I put the question to him: 'What went wrong?'

'I think there was too much Italian immigration,' confided my host, whose ancestors were Spanish. 'They didn't want to fit in, you see, and they began stirring up trouble. It all started to fall apart under Perón.'

There was still considerable residual wealth in Argentina, but it moved in ever decreasing circles. While a select few dined at the Jockey Club and attended polo matches at the Hurlingham, the regional riots and lootings, the shanty towns huddled under bridges, bore witness to a greater national malaise. Two million people in Buenos Aires now occupied the slums or 'misery towns'. Thirteen million Argentines lived in housing that was officially classed as inadequate. The middle classes doubled their working hours and still they struggled to keep face.

And what of the great British railways that once roved across the vast country? Here was one of the most potent symbols of decay. Most of the regional lines had closed now, and the infrastructure was well past repair. The capital's stations, which had once been like palaces of industry, with sweeping staircases, brass fittings and mahogany furniture, were now subsumed into a world of petty crime and black-market enterprise. In one station, there was a mural of two British gentlemen in tailcoats congratulating one another on the arrival of the first train on a new route. But near it, on the dirty ground, Bolivian women crouched selling sweets, plastic toys and bras. Music blasting from dozens of transistor radios created a cacophonous echo in the vaulted roof. The elegant ladies' waiting room was locked, and the table and chairs inside it bore the dust of many years' neglect. These days, railway stations were places to find the most exotic imported pornographic magazines. Shanty towns clung to their embankments like piggybackers. Thieves and beggars prowled along the platforms. Many people believed them too dangerous to use at all.

'Watch out you don't get raped,' said Raquel, when I set off for the suburbs one Sunday morning. I had been invited for lunch at a traditional *quinta*, a colonial-style house with a large garden and orchard, belonging to an elderly upper-class couple. Raquel thought I should take a taxi, but, since I insisted on going by train, she suggested I borrow her mobile telephone. I turned down the offer.

'It might be difficult to fend off a rapist and make a call at the same time,' I reasoned. 'Especially if I keep getting crossed lines.'

'That's a distinct possibility,' Raquel agreed.

If the railway station was somewhere to be robbed or raped, it was also evidently a place where people disappeared. At the booth where I bought my ticket, there were two notices advertising the loss of geriatrics. 'Eighty-five years old,' said one, 'answers to Pepe, balding, forgetful, may be disorientated.' A loony face grinned out of the attached photograph. Pepe must have boarded one of those dangerous trains, never to be seen again.

I found the train I thought was probably going my way, but asked a passenger if it was the right one, to be sure. 'Who knows? The system's out of control!' she cried, more shrilly than I would have expected from her amenable looks. The woman extrapolated rapidly from the dire state of the railways to the city, the country and even the Vatican. Fearing that I had tapped into an infinite source of discontent, I tried to smile my way out of the conversation. Finally I was able to pass it, like a howling baby, to another, more indulgent passenger.

In the twenty minutes or so before the train was due to leave, it filled rapidly – not just with passengers, but with the people who hoped to make money out of them. A troop of sellers and beggars processed through the carriages hawking boxes of chocolate almonds, perfumes, kitchen knives, geometry sets and the ubiquitous fondue sets. Each one gave a short presentation to his captive audience, beginning formally: 'Señoras y señores'. The sellers' strategy was to be noisy and enthusiastic as they commended the marvellous value of the biscuits, the terrific gift-potential of the fondue set.

With nothing to sell, the beggars made a quieter presentation, of their misery, speaking in a low murmur about their joblessness, their children's illnesses and the high cost of medicine. While the hawkers distributed merchandise around the carriage for the perusal of would-be buyers, the beggars circulated misspelt notes briefly summarising their misfortunes. It was thus possible to find yourself juggling fondue sets, chocolate almonds, dyslexic appeals for money, woollen socks – and all this perhaps while a neighbouring passenger investigated your pockets.

Finally, the train ground out of the station with its carnival load of salesmen, beggars, thieves and rapists. On board, the show went on. A Falklands veteran wept in the doorway as he described the psychological damage that made it impossible for him to get a job, before passing around rulers printed with 'Las Malvinas Son

Argentinas'. Small children in ragged clothes distributed pictures of the Virgin Mary with notes attesting to their hunger or poverty. There was a deaf boy who made his appeal in sign-language, having first provided the passengers with typed transcripts of it. A man with no legs hurtled down the aisle on a wheeled wooden platform, collecting coins with the speed and dexterity of one who was used to make his living in trains. Like well-behaved schoolchildren, all facing forward, the passengers paid equal attention to each claimant and, though no fondue sets were sold in my carriage, quite a few Virgins were.

Our train never exceeded an apologetic chug, so there was ample opportunity to take in the scenery, which was of a peculiar desolation. As we left the station we had passed side-lines that were filled with the skeletons of abandoned carriages. Now we were skirting shanty towns. A gang of long-limbed children running beside the track could almost keep pace with the rickety train and, when we finally gained on them, one of the boys stopped to hurl a small rock that glanced off the frame of my open window. 'An inch the other way', I thought absently, 'and that could have killed me.' It struck me then how easy it was to die in a country like Argentina – how unnatural, almost, it was to survive.

The buildings backing on to the tracks bore a political graffiti which seemed to be decades old, since it made complicated allegations about traitors to Perón. *I shall return and be millions!* was scrawled along the hoardings. Argentina was too preoccupied with thoughts about what might have been, I decided. It was funny that a country obsessed by memory was always forgetting or, worse, misremembering history.

This beaten-up old train was sure to join the skeletons on the sidings soon. In the meantime, we were a restless band of lost souls, travelling on a ghost-train through a haunted landscape. At each station we entered the train sounded an eerie whistle, summoning more souls on board. People jumped on and off through the doors, which were never closed between stops. Pickpockets made off with their haul, fresh salesmen and beggars appeared to replenish the dwindling stock. After an hour or so, my turn to jump down from the train came.

The train departed, bound for the pampa, and I crossed the tracks to find myself in a dusty, quintessentially South American town. Most of the houses were one storey, though where the owners could afford it they had added a second or even a third floor. There was a noise of motorbikes and the bossy flashing of 'Drink Coca-Cola' signs, but there was also a sense of that desire for order that is universally suburban. Somebody had placed a palm cross in the front window, a tentative evangelism, or perhaps the intention was simply to reassure passers-by that the future was not altogether hopeless.

I walked through the town, past bungalows and gardens that grew gradually in size and confidence, demanding a larger share of the block until each property had one to itself. Finally I arrived at a large wrought-iron gate and rang the bell. A maid and dog came flying out of the house together. The maid questioned me suspiciously, the dog accompanying her with growls until my presence was deemed incontrovertible, then she directed me through the garden and to open french windows. 'The Señora is in the sitting room,' she said.

I found Elsie, my hostess, sitting in her nightdress on an old leather sofa. 'Come in, dear,' she said. 'I haven't got dressed yet because I got engrossed in some letters from the 1950s.'

The villa was also engrossed in the past. Examples of antique South American art hung on the walls. In the kitchen, among ancient electrical equipment, there was a wall covered in photographs, showing a distant, social world that had ended before the advent of colour photography. There were women in fur capes and plumed hats, groups of people smiling at drinks parties and literary events. Through an open door into the garden, I glimpsed Elsie's husband sitting in a wheelchair staring into nothing, or maybe staring back into that world. Among pictures of various prominent Argentines, there was one of Borges.

'Poor Borges,' said Elsie, joining me at the wall, once she had dressed. 'His mother adored his father, but he was a philanderer, you know. So she invented a fictional happy marriage, a utopia of love which was very difficult for Borges to live up to. As a result, he was always seeking a perfect love, which of course doesn't exist. He dreamed up women, dreamed up life. Borges lived in the air. What do you suppose we could eat for lunch?'

She began opening cupboards and pulling out little tins of fish and potato salad. 'I brought you some chocolate almonds,' I confessed. It occurred to me now that this was an inappropriate present for a couple of eighty-five and ninety years old. But Elsie's eyes lit up at the gift. We took the almonds, tins, wine and bread to an outside table which had once been the scene of literary gatherings.

It was hot again and a low-flying plane bullied the afternoon with announcements for discount sales in local shops. Tranquillity was not something one could protect in South America. Silence was golden, certainly, but only for the politicians and advertisers who leaped to fill it with their own noise. Sometimes I thought that was what I hated most in Argentina: the impossibility of calm.

Now the plane circling Elsie's garden was broadcasting an appeal for a lost dog. It was curious how often dogs disappeared in Buenos Aires. Their grieving owners attached pathetic notes to lamp-posts, instinctively returning to the loved one's old haunts, just as the lost geriatrics' relatives left notices near the pornography stands in railway stations. I had heard a rumour that there were dog-snatching bands at work in the capital, but the wealthy still entrusted their purebreds to professional dog-walkers. These young men, tangled up in dogs like the foxes at the Jockey Club, provided one of the best comic sights in Buenos Aires.

'Borges' mother was not alone,' Elsie was saying. 'We all build stories around ourselves, don't we? We all have imaginary utopias. We decide to be sexy or distinguished.'

'I suppose we do. What did you decide to be?'

'I decided to be English.'

Elsie was really of Eastern European extraction, but she had fallen in love with English culture as a young girl, when she met a smart employee of the English Land Company, travelling through

Patagonia. The story was a paradigm: here was the Englishman Mr Taylor offering an oasis of civilisation in the midst of the wilderness. I imagined him to be an archetypal gentleman, handsome and courteous, perhaps a hat-doffer. Smitten, Elsie had started reading English magazines and, at sixteen, she persuaded her family to let her do a secretarial course in Croydon, which she found 'frivolous but rewarding'. In London she had met her husband.

'The English really *invented* Argentina,' Elsie said. 'Their culture used to be so important here, but nowadays the depreciation is painful. Few people are loyal to the ways of the British, and they're letting the traditions die out. People only learn English for commercial reasons.'

She listed the many times she had written to the British Council to complain about this state of affairs, each time being rudely fobbed off or ignored. Elsie's husband was mostly silent during the meal but every now and then little hiccups of indignation burst from him.

'What does it matter to you, woman?' he spluttered. 'Why do you mind so much about these things?'

'I'm eighty-five and I'm keeping my neurones alive. Don't criticise me or you won't get any cake.'

Many Argentines loved the English, but Elsie belonged to a class whose passion for Englishness was an article of faith, indicating a precise set of beliefs not about England, but about Argentina. These Anglophiles – Borges was one of them – abhorred Perón and made it a point of honour to call Evita a prostitute. Elsie was true to form in this respect. In a perfect, succinct and scathing English, she tore into many sacred cows of the left.

'This business of the disappeared is greatly exaggerated – it's one of our great myths, like the myth that Evita was a friend of the poor and that Kennedy was a magnificent democrat. The trouble is, this country is hooked on clichés. No one ever speaks about the torture that took place under Perón. No, the really guilty people were not the military but the families who allowed their children to become delinquents.'

'Do you not even believe the official figure of disappeared?' I asked. The National Commission on Disappeared People's estimate of 8,960 was considered conservative by most people.

'No, of course not.'

After lunch, we walked around the *quinta*'s diminished grounds. Elsie told me that once there had been a bigger garden and orchard, but they had been obliged to sell land for development. Terrorists had chased them out of their holiday home in Uruguay and she wondered how much longer they would be able to afford the upkeep of the *quinta*. She measured, for me, the extent of their financial decline in bathrooms. 'Once we had seven, now we have only three.'

'Do you like Buenos Aires?' I asked.

'Of course. It's a fascinating city, the disorder allows you to do so much. Life is so exigent in Europe now, everyone is concerned with staying alive and they have no time or money to waste. I make a point of wasting time. Would you pick those up for me?' She poked at some avocados lying in the long grass.

'Perhaps you wouldn't like England if you could see it now.'

'Of course I would.' She was rather too assertive, I thought, for one who wanted to be English. 'England has changed, but not enough to lose its essence. Anyway, it survives all over the world. Indira Gandhi was one of the finest Englishwomen I ever met.'

'Even so, it must be very different—'

'I love England,' she interrupted. 'I love England.'

Two of the most interesting people I met in Buenos Aires worked in cemeteries. Perhaps that should not be surprising in a country where death was so significant. In Argentina, once you were dead, you were rarely buried – coffined bodies were stored above ground in mausoleums, or in walls of niches – and certainly not forgotten. Anniversaries pertaining to the deceased continued to be observed. 'The living are so dead in Buenos Aires because the dead are so alive,' complained Uki Goñi. People who worked among the unburied dead might be expected to have evolved a unique outlook on philosophy, history and the meaning of life.

Carlos Menéndez, a pall-bearer and grave-digger at Chacarita, where Perón was buried, gave me briefings on political and economic history. 'It would have been much better if the British had succeeded in their 1806 invasion,' he said. 'We were an informal British colony anyway, in economic terms, but we never reaped the full rewards of cultural association with Britain. We inherited a Latin temperament, and look where it got us.' Carlos, whose fingertips were darkened by soil and tobacco, told me he read books by British and American historians, but never by Argentines.

It was fascinating to see the bureaucracy of death at work in Chacarita. In a reception building at the front of the cemetery, people formed weary queues to deposit or collect ashes, to make enquiries about burials or cremations. Like queuers anywhere else in the city, they smoked and complained, fanning themselves impatiently with their forms. They made the same sort of quips, but with deathly undertones. 'Next thing they'll be telling us we can't get into heaven without the right form,' said one man.

Chacarita's lugubrious system decreed that a coffin could be placed in a niche, but only for fifteen years, after which it was required to be buried underground. Even then, after twenty-five years' burial, the body must be exhumed and cremated, so that the process of resting in peace could take forty years. Relatives often liked to accompany their loved ones on to the next stage of this cycle. 'Sometimes they want to open up the coffins to have a quick look at the deceased,' said Carlos. 'It's morbid, but I suppose they're curious.'

The other enlightened grave-tender in my life was Hugo Palavecino, who looked after Evita's tomb, among others. After our first meeting, we had stood for an hour or so, literally over Evita's dead body, discussing history and literature. We became friends and every so often I went to look for him in the cemetery. We would pick a sunny spot somewhere in the labyrinth of tombs and talk about books and plants, which were Hugo's passion. He was a particular admirer of W. H. Hudson; the thought of the ailing writer languishing in an Earl's Court boarding house while he yearned for Patagonia moved him deeply.

'What I find hard to forgive is that so few people came to this country with a vision of its future,' Hugo told me one afternoon. 'They came to get rich quick. Some people arrived poor from Europe and made great fortunes but, even though they lived in Argentina, they spoke of Spain and Italy as home and they spent months of every year in Europe.'

Since these early looters lay all around us, Hugo voiced his recriminations quietly. 'The very people who founded Argentina and had a chance to shape the country had no ideals. If you're going to live in a place, you have to make a commitment to it. You have to love it the way you love a woman.'

Every now and then a funeral procession crossed one of the innumerable intersections within our sights and suddenly there would be a glimpse of a splendid mahogany coffin, decked in flowers and followed by richly dressed mourners. The apparition vanished, then a flash of sun on brass drew the eye to another intersection and there it was again, then again somewhere else, as the procession snaked its way through the labyrinth to a final resting place.

'Does that ever depress you', I asked, 'death?'

'Not at all,' said Hugo. 'I'm among friends here.' Hugo had worked at Recoleta for more than thirty years, since his boyhood, and in that time many of his clients had died and joined their families in the tombs he serviced. So the dead were indeed companionable.

'Death doesn't frighten me, except to make me feel that life is ephemeral. I'm shocked by the speed at which time passes. Twenty years have gone by in a flash and there are so many things I would have liked to do.'

Once Hugo took me on a guided tour of Recoleta. We squinted in the sun at a skyline of cupolas and crucifixes. Hugo pointed out his favourite angels, three elderly men with long pointed wings, who sat sadly surveying the waste of death around them. He told me that the marble relief of a girl escaping through an open door had been erected by distraught parents whose daughter had been buried alive. At night, the girl had come out of a coma, and workers had heard her knocking on the coffin's lid, but, by the time they could retrieve a key to the mausoleum, she had suffocated. Here was a case where the 'missing key' had proved fatal. 'Nowadays we make sure to keep copies,' said Hugo.

Many of the coffins at Recoleta lay in full view of people who came every day to lay wreaths, to say prayers, or simply to peer at them. The corpses could not be seen, yet the proximity of legendary bones offered a frisson. Here was General Rosas, the notorious Caudillo whose remains had only recently been repatriated from Southampton, where he died. Rosas was still controversial in Argentina. He had succeeded in uniting the country in the mid nineteenth century, but the price was a campaign of terror that set a bloody precedent in Argentine history. Citizens found not wearing the red ribbon of allegiance to Rosas risked having their throats cut by his ruthless death squad.

On the other side of the cemetery lay Sarmiento, the great liberal thinker and sworn enemy of Rosas who succeeded him as president in 1868. Sarmiento's famous denunciation of Rosas' regime was a classic book, an historic appeal to Argentines to follow the route of 'Civilisation' as epitomised by the city, rather than the 'Barbarism' of the gauchos on the pampa. Ever since Sarmiento, Argentines had been troubled by this dualism at the heart of their identity. Perhaps that was why *porteños* were so sophisticated. Their European cafés were a buffer against the primitive pampa. Their weekly manicure staved off barbarism.

Life-long enemies were joined in death at the Recoleta. In a low tomb, hidden from public view, lay the remains of President Aramburu, summarily executed by Montoneros for his part in the abduction of Evita's body. Aramburu's indignities had not ended with his death; his body was held ransom for Evita's. Yet not far from Aramburu lay Evita herself. Hugo told me that he often visited her sisters.

'They find it very hard to deal with all that's happened,' he said. 'They're permanently dazed by it.'

'Who is the worst villain in the cemetery?' I asked.

'There must be a few,' he said, 'but it isn't right to speak ill of the dead.'

Though Recoleta was one of the capital's great architectural treasures, and certainly its top tourist site, the tombs were left to determine their own life-span. Coffins placed in niches were subject to the same cycle of burial and cremation as in Chacarita, but the splendid mausoleums were sold to families in perpetuity. They could not be touched by the cemetery's administrator, even if the family died out and the walls began to crumble. Through the broken doors of one little chapel, I saw an altar covered in rubble and, lying among it, plastic flowers and the scattered feathers of a dead bird. Elsewhere, coffins lurched out of broken niches threatening to spill their load of bodies into the alleys. In some corners of the cemetery, there was a distinct smell of putrefaction. Civilisation and barbarism fought for dominance among the tombs. An army of cats sought to oppress an uprising of rats.

One afternoon, Hugo drove me to the city of La Plata, because he wanted me to see the famous Natural History Museum where there were important examples of dinosaur remains. I thought it was funny that we were leaving one repository of dead tyrants' bones to go to another.

The museum was practically deserted and I was conscious of the noise of my shoes on the tiles as we strolled among the skeletons. After the dinosaurs, we went to look at mammals, passing under the massive skeleton of a whale. We were admiring a selection of birds and mountain animals, beautifully preserved and boxed, when Hugo said:

'Do you think there's a chance for a better life?'

'You mean, in Argentina?'

'No. I mean after death. Is there a better world after this one?'

'You're the one to know. What do you think?'

'I don't know,' he said. 'But I want to believe that there is.'

CHAPTER EIGHT

Cake-fighting in Patagonia, and Other Travels

THE OLD LADY in the room upstairs was dying. She had been dying at least since that morning, when I had arrived at the little boarding house in the Andes, and for all I knew she had been dying for months or even years before that. In South America things took time, and people were used to waiting. They waited in supermarkets and at the bank. They waited on dusty roadsides for buses that were hours late. They waited for the truth about their disappeared, for a change of government, hanging on for *mañana*, for a better life or an afterlife.

The woman upstairs was simply waiting to die. All day she had been singing, in a sweet, frail voice, about the mystery of her death. 'I'm going, I'm going – but where to?' Each time she repeated the mantra, she slightly altered the arrangement of words, as if testing a combination lock for entry to the next world. 'Where am I going? When am I going? Why?'

Soothed by the shifting pattern of words, I lay in bed and tried to feel well, or at any rate not quite so ill. Yet every part of my body conspired against this positive attitude. I must have been suffering from half a dozen maladies, including a virulent stomach infection, 'flu and scabies. A living itch occupied the strip of flesh, around both ankles, where parasites had recently found an entry point between my trousers and socks. I had consulted a pharmacist earlier in the day, between fits of vomiting, who warned me that they would 'migrate' should I fail to apply his foul-smelling lotion to my entire body every few hours. It was dispiriting to think of my body as an expanse large enough for migrations; during these last unhappy hours of immobility, I had come to imagine myself as a continent across which microscopic creatures were roaming like gauchos on the pampa.

The light was fading outside and a mountain chill gripped the air. The owner of the boarding house had lent me an electric fire, insinuating, as she did so, that it might be dangerous to use. I dared not take that risk, so I lay, fully dressed, beneath the huddle of blankets, shivering and sweating myself out of the fever. I had eaten nothing all day, taking only a little coca-leaf tea, to counter the effects of the altitude. I was a long way, now, from Buenos Aires with its regime of catastrophes and crossed wires, the haunting black-and-white faces of the disappeared. I could remember the absurd argument I had once had about vegetables in a library and laugh to myself, though in the circumstances laughing was rather painful.

I was in Peru and – it almost made me smile to think of it – I was on assignment. In fact I had already accomplished my mission, which was to spend some days living with a group of Indians on the Uros Islands in the Peruvian part of Lake Titicaca. The Uros were forty floating islands, man-made from the *totora* reeds which grew in the water around them. No one knew when or why the islands had first appeared in the lake, though it was said that they dated to the time of the Spanish conquest, and possibly further back. The original inhabitants were rumoured to have been chased off the mainland by the Incas, as a punishment for their laziness.

The 300 or so Aymara Indians who now inhabited the islands led most precarious lives. The reeds they lived on were always rotting – and it could be fatal to fall into the icy waters of the lake – so they were bound to dedicate most of their waking hours to the wearisome business of maintaining their islands' fabric. It was the men's job to collect reeds and, when the nearer sources were depleted, they had to strike deep into the lake, sometimes undertaking two-day missions in search of this crucial plant. Every aspect of the islanders' lives depended on *totora*: they made their huts and boats from it, they used it as fuel and even ate it, in its greenest state. The mystical existence of the islanders frightened their neighbours on the mainland, who imagined that they must have superhuman powers.

The life of the Uros islanders, their subjugation to the exhausting cycle of rotting and replenishment, was well worth writing about, but since my article was for a glossy women's magazine I was obliged to focus on their private lives. Sex was a priority for most editors nowadays and mine had given me to understand that I could consider myself a failure if I returned from Peru without knowledge of the women's sexual liaisons and menstrual cycles. 'Intimate detail' was specified in my contract. 'Just make sure you get the story,' I had been warned. Evidently, the competition for good, sex-based stories was tough in London. Lying in bed, fighting the temptation to scratch my ravaged ankles, I found myself resenting the jaded com-muters who had to be entertained on the tube with stories of other people's sex lives.

On arrival in Peru, I had managed to arrange my sojourn on the floating islands through a local guide who knew the inhabitants and wisely suggested that we approach the Mothers' Club on the biggest island. Women's groups were often the focus of indigenous com-munities in the Andes. My guide had introduced me to 24-year-old Rosa, president of the Mothers' Club on the biggest island, Tribuna. Before my visit could be officially approved, I was taken into the mothers' meeting-hut, and sat down in the centre of a group of some thirty women and girls. La Presidenta had laid down the conditions for my stay: she would require a sack of bread rolls and another of bananas to be distributed among the mothers, as well as a supply of school exercise books and wool. There was to be bubblegum too. The women's passion for gum was evident in that most wore a piece stuck inside the rim of their hats. The splendid

Derby hat, with or without its gum adornment, was an essential feature of Aymara women's dress.

Once the details of my visit were finalised, the women had taken turns to ask me questions, including some of the intimate ones I had been shy of putting to them. Those who spoke Spanish translated for the ones who understood only Aymara. Did I have a boyfriend, they wondered, and where was he? Did I have children? How did I achieve the whiteness of my skin?

'How old are you?' someone asked.

'Twenty-seven.'

For some reason this answer caused hilarity in the hut and several of the women broke into excited Aymara. I felt suddenly vulnerable, sitting in the middle of the hut as foreign laughter rippled around me.

'What are you saying?' I asked, nervous of their amusement.

'You don't look nearly so old,' said one of the women. 'We thought you were about fifteen.'

'Am I going? Where am I going to? Where am I going to go? Where am I going to go to?'

Footsteps travelled across the ceiling. 'Be quite, *mamacita*,' came a voice, sympathetic but firm. 'You're not going anywhere, dear, you're staying here with us.'

I rushed to the bathroom to expel the coca tea. The vomiting relieved my stomach, but the misery of the act increased the ache in my bones. Old and pained, I crept back between the sheets. Nostalgia, so much harder to fight when matched to illness, rushed in where nausea had abated. I tried to imagine that I was lying in an English garden on a summer's day, a scent of roses and honeysuckle in the air, the tinkle and chat of Pimm's drinkers assuaging my ears and, perhaps, in the distance, the music of a fountain. The fantasy was too exaggerated: my fever refused to feed it. I moved on to one side and felt, with some satisfaction, the tear that had collected in one eye roll over my nose and on to the pillow. The thought that I was alone in the Peruvian Andes, with a dying neighbour and an unspecified number of nomadic parasites as my only company, conjured more tears.

In the end, I had spent two days with La Presidenta, sleeping in her one-room hut with her family, under her scabies-infested blankets, also under the leery eye of her husband, who was fascinated to know if I was comfortable. I was, as far as it was possible to be, when only a clutch of rotting reeds separated me from the fatal waters of the world's highest lake. At night the water was quite still, though like the princess's pea it communicated all its cold through however many layers of blankets I slept upon. At one point during the night, an island dog shot past the hut, causing the ground to give slightly, and I felt the water swell ominously underneath me.

Fortunately, the women had turned out to be loquacious on the subject of boyfriends and periods, as we sat untangling fishing nets together. On my last night they had dressed me in the traditional outfit of the Aymara woman, a wide skirt, shawl and Derby hat, and we had danced – carefully – to the crackling music of their transistor radio. I had thought, with wonder: 'Will anything like this ever happen to me again?' It seemed so extraordinary to be dancing with Indians on top of the world, feeling the water heave under my feet. Before I left the island, I became godmother to several children and La Presidenta thought I might be more useful still.

'Why don't you marry one of our men and share your wealth with him?' she had suggested.

I had sidestepped the marriage, but I did get the story, complete with intimate detail. Did that make me a foreign correspondent? No – the idea was absurd. I knew a number of correspondents in South America, most of them determined men and women who hankered after scoops and revolutions. From time to time, they congregated in hotel rooms in that moment's newsworthy part of the continent, and spoke cagily about their work and the stories they were chasing. I lingered, curious, at the margin of their conversations about fugitive Nazis and Brazilian death-squads, but my instinct was to run away from a story, rather than chase it, and I knew that I was lousy at my job. I was happier sitting in cemeteries, discussing Graham Greene with grave-diggers than 'breaking news'.

Night fell. It was too cold to undress, but I decided to invoke the comforting ritual of bedtime by swapping some of my garments for others. I cleaned my face and teeth and returned to bed. While I was in the bathroom some men had gathered in the courtyard and were now standing close to my window, laughing and whispering about a woman. I hoped, with a horror, that I was not the source of their excited amusement. Earlier in the day, when I had made my dash to the pharmacist, I had seen three men lingering in the courtyard and noticed that each of them had one front tooth framed in gold. This was a popular dental accessory with both men and women in the Andes, but somehow it did not inspire confidence. The presence of gold insinuated a motive into what might otherwise have been a well-meaning smile. There was no chance of sleep, I told myself, until the men moved away from my window.

At length they did move, but I could not sleep anyway. In fact I felt too restless even to close my eyes. Instead I lay staring pointlessly into the night, wondering about all the things I had done with my life and what I would do in the future, how happy I had been and would be. I wondered how long I would live, and if I would die in South America. I lay in the dark, wondering and worrying about all these things for hours, a silent witness to my neighbour's swan-song. She must have been really determined to die, because she went on testing combinations throughout the night.

We travelled, together or apart, as often as we could, crisscrossing the continent on trains and buses that were always breaking down (in that sense, at least, they were reliable). We grew used to travelling among chickens and Indian children with swirls of dirt and mucus trailing from their nostrils, or on the backs of farmers' trucks transporting sacks of potatoes or bananas to market. On the overnight buses, we were shown videos of a remarkable, blood-chilling violence. One night I woke up in a coach that had broken down in the

Bolivian Andes. A group of men had gathered around the engine, scratching their heads and looking dangerously baffled. The drunks sleeping in the gangway began to stir under their ponchos. There was only one other woman on the bus and she was being bludgeoned to death, on the video.

Some South American drivers treated their buses as extensions of their homes, lovingly decorating them with photographs, talismans and the inevitable rosary or plastic madonna swinging from the rear-view mirror. They might also be vehicles of proselytisation: often there were half a dozen or more printed postcards stuck above the windows, bearing maxims about the importance of working hard, being kind to your neighbours and remembering God. Other post-cards bore the same jokes about sex, money and mothers-in-law that you might see in an English pub, but with the necessary adjustments made for this language's different innuendo and rhyme. It crossed my mind that there might be an international supplier of such humour; perhaps a team of translators laboured to make mothers-in-law funny in every corner of the world.

I met people who were searching for things and others who were running from things, importers collecting artefacts and missionaries disseminating religion. On one bumpy journey across the Peruvian high plain, I sat next to Ernesto, a Marxist from Lima who was planning a revolution, though he assured me that it would not be a violent one. He was proud to own the same name as Ernesto 'Che' Guevara and I was tempted to make a joke about the importance of being Ernest, but guessed it might not be appreciated by my serious companion.

Elsewhere, a Chilean poet offered to write a poem about my eyes – for money – and in Ecuador I met a young Californian, called Cindy, who was searching for herself. Cindy described herself as 'Unitedstatesian', because she did not wish to offend the continent's other inhabitants by appropriating 'American' for one, selfish country. She was worried about Washington's imperialism, the rights of animals and, more specifically, about a boyfriend who had told her he loved her but that he needed space. She had given him the whole state of California, while she travelled for six months in Latin America. Cindy struck me as being prone to unnecessary anxiety. Back in California, she told me, she was taking an evening class on domestic violence.

Some of the travellers I met had given up jobs and even homes to explore South America. What were they looking for? Many had simple requirements: they would return home with an alpaca jumper and some cheap jewellery, a few entertaining anecdotes about illnesses and corrupt policemen. Others, it seemed, really were looking for the meaning of life in the ancient cultures of Bolivia or Peru. Tall and healthy, they strode among the locals in the bustling streets of Quito and La Paz, confident in their shorts and T-shirts, but with the quizzical expression of someone who cannot remember what it is he has forgotten. The indigenous people watched them with awe, as if they were gods.

As I travelled, I came to know the neuroses and passions of the different nations that made up Latin America. Just as Argentina cherished the injustice of the Falklands, so each country had a grievance which its citizens were encouraged to nurse from an early age. Chileans laid claim to a part of the Argentine Andes. Ecuadoreans hated Peru for pinching some of the jungle. Bolivia had lost its coastline to Chile in 1879 and now Bolivian officials sat under posters which showed a foamy sea lapping on to a sandy shore: 'This Is Our Sea'. 'I am one of the lucky few who has seen our sea,' a Bolivian librarian told me. 'If only more of my brothers and sisters could see how beautiful it is, I think that they would try harder to get it back.'

Every Latin American country nurtured a dream, the elusive promise of a great future, and on every street corner there was a two-bit philosopher ready with a reason for his country's failure. It was the fault of the Spaniards, the corruption, the International Monetary Fund, the Americans. 'Our poverty is essential to your success,' a man with a stabbing figure told me. 'Westerners don't want to share their money.'

In the nineteenth century, the liberator Simón Bolívar, the continent's greatest dreamer, envisioned a powerful Latin American federation that would rival the United States, but his dream had foundered, as the continent fell to fighting. 'We have ploughed the sea,' Bolívar lamented, on his death-bed.

'Where am I going? When am I going? Why am I going?'

I must briefly have fallen asleep, because I woke up to find myself vigorously scratching my ankles. I opened my eyes and such a blackness leaned on them that my heart quickened. I closed them again, though with the petulant conviction that I would never sleep.

Once we had taken a coach to Jujuy, a city close to Argentina's northern border. The journey lasted nearly twenty-four hours, but I enjoyed the enforced calm of the coach as it travelled smoothly through the flatlands; the empty landscape was soothing on the eye and the mind. Two men shared the driving to Bolivia, one long-legged and the other short, with a perfectly round belly that looked as if it had been pressed out of a pudding mould on to his otherwise lean body. While one drove, the other dispensed, every two hours or so, plastic cups of Coca-Cola and large round biscuits glued together with *dulce de leche*, a caramel spread to which many Argentines were addicted. I had once read that the dying General Perón had to be bribed with *dulce de leche* before he would sign documents.

The three television sets posted along the gangway carried alternate videos of romance and extreme violence. The drivers must have thought that a democratic arrangement, sure to please both sexes, or perhaps it was simply that one driver liked romance, while the other relished violence. The long-legged one, lolloping back and forth with trays, looked more the romantic type to me. As the hours passed, I watched the fertile pampa gradually become tinged with red before finally surrendering to the arid north. The setting sun seeped over the vast horizon in sympathy with the landscape's vivid reds.

From Jujuy we had taken a local bus to Abra Pampa, a derelict Andean mining town in what was now one of the very poorest regions of Argentina. We had been invited to meet some Spanish monks who were working with the destitute there. Most of the men in the town were unemployed tin miners, living with their families in adobe huts; illness and malnutrition were rife among the children. Health and education services were very poor. The sight of men and women trudging down the town's ill-lit dirt street conveyed all the blighted despondency of a Lowry painting.

In the monks' frugal living room we had huddled around a gas stove. 'People in Buenos Aires have no idea what life is like here,' one of them said. 'It's all very well the government asking Argentines to tighten their belts, but here it's impossible: there are simply no more notches.' He had laughed and tipped back in his seat, as if to show us a belt that could not be further tightened. Later, the monks served us a Spanish supper of potato omelette, ham and red wine and spoke of their home, which they were allowed to visit every seven years, and of how they had come to work in this forgotten corner of Argentina.

Afterwards we walked back down the dirt street to the boarding house and went to bed early, like the town's other inhabitants: there was nothing in Abra Pampa to stay up for, after all. Then, some hours later, I woke suddenly, subject to another one of those night-shocks, except that this time it was not a vision of plummeting lifts or asphyxiating babies that had wakened me, gasping. I *really* could not breathe. My throat seemed to have closed over and my heart and head were pounding an alarm together. I realised that I must be suffering from altitude sickness and, panicking, I thought that I was going to die. There was a door from our room into a patio and I rushed outside in my nightdress and lay down on the ground, painfully breathless, like Evita when she thought of the poor. Struggling to calm my breathing but also to breathe enough, I stretched out my arms and pressed myself against the earth, as if this connection with nature would sway whatever balance my life hung in. As I fought to draw the necessary air into my lungs, I stared at the Andean sky and at the magnificent array of stars hinting at infinity. That was the first time I noticed that there was an unfamiliar face on the full moon quivering above me. The southern moon hung upside down.

Some time during my long night in the Peruvian boarding house, the woman upstairs must have found the combination she needed for, as dawn broke, I heard her frail voice call out: 'I know where I'm going. I know now. I know.' That was the last of her song. A silence reigned when I got up an hour or so later. The parasitic itch had calmed considerably by then and I assumed that the migration had been halted, though both my ankles looked battle-scarred – in fact the scars would last for several months. My stomach felt better too, so there was only the 'flu to contend with. I showered, got dressed and prepared to make my way, by train, bus and plane, back to Buenos Aires – back home, as I sometimes thought of it.

Patagonia was famous for nothing so much as its wind. Gerald Durrell, who otherwise loathed his time working for the British Council in Argentina, was haunted by it. Bruce Chatwin, vainly hitching his way across the treeless wastes, was tormented by its cruel imitation of approaching lorries. Native Patagonians were fond of attributing sirens' powers to their wind. It could permanently damage you, they hinted. It could stay with you for ever.

And semi-mystical powers had also been attributed to Marta Rees' exquisite ice-cream cake, the *pièce de résistance* of an enormous Welsh tea served up to tourists at her tea house in Gaiman, in eastern Patagonia. 'You can learn how to make a cake or ice it, but the essence of a cake, that can never be taught,' said Marta. 'It's something you have to have inside.'

Though the wind might howl its ghoulish worst outside, Marta's kitchen was a picture of familial cosiness. Tea towels from Wales hung on the walls alongside completed jigsaws of Welsh landscapes; an outsize kettle was permanently on the hob. The flickering television picture of gaudy blondes hosting game shows was the only hint that this was Argentina.

Marta was in her seventies, a small woman with dark, wild hair that seemed to sense the power of the wind prowling outside. A direct descendant of the original 160 colonisers who arrived in Patagonia from Wales in 1865 she looked Welsh, spoke Welsh, and let her mind wander every now and then to those green hills and valleys a world away.

Over plates loaded with bread and cake, Marta told us how her mother-in-law had opened Ty Plas y Coed in 1930, to provide sustenance for the country people coming into town from the Welsh farms on market days. Dilys Owen Jones was a great cook, and word about her amazing cakes quickly swept Patagonia. Evidently she was a big-hearted woman too, who did not want to charge her friends for tea, but they insisted on giving her something – and that was how teas became a business in Gaiman. Dilys had considered herself a good Patagonian and a good Argentine. Hanging in the tea room was a framed certificate from the Argentine government, thanking her for a life of 'hard work and affection'.

Thanks to her mother-in-law's enterprise, Marta could claim to run the oldest tea house in Gaiman. This was an important boast, for there were five tea houses competing for the business of tourists who came to visit the Welsh settlement. Throughout the year, but especially during the European and American summer holiday season, a steady flow of visitors was available to sample Gaiman's cakes. 'Twenty years ago some boy called Chadwick came here, and then wrote a book,' said Marta. 'My husband said not to bother reading it, because it was all wrong, but I must say, I've had a lot of custom thanks to him.'

Gaiman was a neat, leafy town – in Britain it might have been eligible for a 'best-kept' contest. Ranged around the grassy main square the tea houses advertised their names on quaint, teapot-shaped signs. There were cakes here to make a gourmand's eyes pop: chocolate cake with banana cream, apple turnover, lemon cake, crème caramel. The famous *torta negra*, a dense, dark fruitcake, was the litmus test of an expert tea. A woman in Gaiman would sooner sell her body than reveal her recipe for *torta negra*.

But there was trouble brewing in the teapots of Gaiman, for a new *luxury* tea house had opened and threatened the livelihood of the other five. The modern tea house looked like a hotel. It had parking for coaches and extensive gardens, offering the perfect surroundings in which to digest *torta negra*. Hymns sung by Welsh male choirs were piped into the salon and even into the lavatory. The Israeli president had caused a ruckus when, visiting Gaiman, he chose this state-of-the-art establishment over the other five for his tea. The worst of it was that the owners were said not even to speak Welsh; they had named the house Ty Caerdydd, even though they had no connection with Cardiff. These were people, Marta might have philosophised, who did not carry the essence of cake-making within them. In fact they employed a chef. Ty Caerdydd was a symptom of what some residents angrily referred to as the 'Welshification' of Gaiman.

'If only they could specialise in one sort of cake each,' sighed Lynned, headmistress of the local school. 'Then people could go to all of them, and there needn't be any conflict.' She had invited us for lunch on Sunday, and it was almost like Sunday lunch in a British rectory. An old upright piano, brought from Wales, sustained a battered dignity in a corner of the sitting room and there were old copies of *The Observer* on the table, which were sent from Wales every three months. We ate roast beef and discussed politics, causing Lynned's husband to wave his arms in exasperation at the head of the table.

Later, we visited Lynned's sister, who ran a local museum, charting the history of the first Welsh settlers. The collection contained a spinning wheel, clothing, and letters which told of the hazards of leaving home for a new and dangerous life.

It was in the 1850s that a group of Welsh nationalists had first set their sights on Patagonia, a region not yet officially held by any government, and inhabited only by Indians. There, freed from the tyranny of English landlords, they hoped to make a 'little Wales beyond Wales', where each family could work its own land and where their language and strict brand of Protestantism could thrive unmolested. Fired by this vision of a future utopia, the Welsh Colonising Society set up to promote emigration to Patagonia grossly exaggerated the suitability of the new land, describing it as 'green and splendid' with 'luscious pastures' and 'tall, strong forests'. The climate was judged to be one of the most agreeable in the world, with temperatures that were 'very pleasant and adaptable to the Welshman's constitution'.

The first group of colonisers to arrive, in 1865, found the region desolate, treeless and bitterly cold. Their huts had to be constructed with materials brought from elsewhere, and then they were washed away by the rains. Strong winds undid the ploughed land; fifty acres of potatoes and maize were lost. By the end of the first year, with no harvest and all the cattle killed or strayed, the settlers wondered if they would even survive in this brutal land. Help came from the government in Buenos Aires which, keen to promote the settlement of Patagonia, agreed a monthly grant. With a resilience that was the stuff of local legend, the Welsh pressed inland until they found good soil in the Chubut valley. They learned hunting and fishing from the Tehuelche Indians. 'The Welsh were always friendly with the Indians, you know,' said Marta. 'It was the Spanish who killed them.'

Little Wales prospered: in 1869 the first successful crop was harvested, and five years later Gaiman, meaning 'sudden village' in Welsh, was founded. The settlers were joined by brethren from Wales and the United States, some of whom pushed on as far west as the Andes. But immigration from Wales had dried up by 1914 and, as Argentina expanded into its own hinterland, the Welsh were swamped by Spanish settlers. By mid-century, to be Welsh was to invite taunts in the school playground. The Welsh language, although it kept a toehold in the choirs and chapels, and some families continued to speak it, was reviled as unpatriotic. Young Patagonians were embarrassed to speak it and, gradually, the language declined.

Today, among the 20,000 Welsh descendants in Patagonia, there were only a few hundred Welsh-speakers left – and they were mostly old. Yet, just as it seemed bound for extinction, Welsh culture was making an extraordinary comeback in Patagonia. A new programme, funded by donations from both sides of the Atlantic, had been sending Welsh-speakers from Wales to teach in Patagonia, and paying for Patagonian students, choirs and musicians to go on study and concert tours in Wales. On a recent exchange visit a number of Patagonian teenagers had fallen in love with their Welsh counterparts, which was judged to be a very good omen.

An early benefiter of the scheme, twenty-eight-year-old Gabriel Restucha, had been to study in Wales, and now he was teaching, at Lynned's school, the first Welsh-language course to receive official recognition in a Patagonian school since the 1880s. 'Even a few years ago, the taboo against speaking the Welsh language was so strong that I didn't know my grandmother spoke it,' said Gabriel Restucha. 'It was emotional the first time we talked in Welsh.' He took us to meet his grandmother and the four of us stood awkwardly around a kitchen table that bore only a raw joint of meat. 'I'm very proud of Gabriel,' said his grandmother.

All of a sudden, in this sudden town, Welshness was wresting back the territory gained by Welshification. Nowadays, even the hippest teenagers made time for choir practice and talked about their plans for the next Eisteddfod. Gruff Finch, who had come from Cardiff to teach Welsh for a year, was delighted by the enthusiasm shown by his pupils, some of whom had no Welsh blood at all.

But he was puzzled by the cake-fighting.

'I don't really know where they got this "tea house" idea from,' said Gruff. 'In Wales we mostly go to cafés, like they do in England and Scotland. It's a shame that the new place is threatening the others, but they do have an excellent chef. I have to say, they make a terrific custard cream.'

'It's luxurious rather than cosy, but, you know, sometimes people *want* the best. You've got to be business-minded,' said María, who ran Ty Caerdydd with her husband. With pretty blonde hair and manicured nails, she was rather too glamorous for Gaiman. We sat, like pilgrims, before a vast tea in the pink opulence of the salon.

María had shown us the genuine bible in a glass case near the door, and the genuine sewing machine and iron. A male chorus swelled from the sound system. Since this was our third tea in two days, it was not welcome – though the custard cream Gruff had recommended was delicious indeed – but María was keen to show that she could keep up with the others. The other tea ladies had not given her a warm reception: only one had agreed to share some cake recipes with her, and no one would reveal the recipe for *torta negra*.

'These ladies are stuck thirty years in the past,' María complained. 'They don't realise that nowadays people want their money's worth – tourists can be very demanding. They may look for tradition, but they want comfort too. We get groups of Japanese here and we've got phones and faxes. We've mastered every detail of the tea-serving, you know, warming the pot and everything, but if we had shabby old curtains and carpets no one would come here.'

María's husband told us how President Roca had stopped to take tea with his ancestors during the campaign to exterminate Indians way back in the 1870s. Miguel Angel had studied tourism and knew that tourists were interested in ecology, so their teas were 'ecological' – all the jams were made with produce from their own organic garden. They were thinking of holding concerts of Welsh music, to accompany the teas.

'I insisted to my husband that the crockery had to be porcelain, never mind the expense,' said María. 'The teapots come from Buenos Aires, they're the very best that money can buy. There's an old lady of eighty who makes cosies and I bought mine from her, in pink and white, although white is problematic because it's difficult to get the stains out.'

By the afternoon, news was out of our visit to the Ty Caerdydd. 'I saw you walking past on your way up to the new place,' said Ada Jones, disapprovingly. 'You haven't even tried one of my teas yet.'

It would be our fourth Welsh tea, our second in one day, but there was no way to turn Ada down. We sat despondently at the kitchen table as plates heavy with cake were prepared and brought to us. As we ate, Ada grilled us on the tea at Ty Caerdydd because, as a matter of principle, she could not go there to sample it herself. We told her about the marble tables, the ecological jams, the sound system. 'How ridiculous – a Welsh tea house should be a homely place, not a palace,' said Ada, refilling the teapot.

We had our fifth and final tea for breakfast at Marta's. She wanted us to try the house speciality, which had not been included in the first tea she gave us. We protested, but she insisted, wild hair brooking no argument: she would not charge us for it, but we must not leave Gaiman without trying her ice-cream cake. We sat eating silently, a pretty Welsh landscape hanging around us in jigsaws and tea towels. Marta stood over us as we ate. Without being presumptuous, she said, she suspected there was nothing to compare with this, her *obra maestra*, at the posh establishment up the road.

Mouths, stomachs, hearts and minds full of cake, we had no option but to agree that she was right.

The bus that took us away from Gaiman contained three requests not to smoke and one not to salivate – but there were no jokes about mothers-in-law. Clint Eastwood, chewing gum with menace on the video, accompanied us on the night-journey across Patagonia to the foothills of the Andes; the howling wind, seeking to unravel sound minds, beat against the sides of the bus. For hours, the plain unfurled, like a video game, a monotonous scene in which the only variety was in the distribution of rocks and boulders. Our driver must have played this game many times before; even so, at some point during the night he lost his last life on a badly negotiated boulder or rut. With a shout of 'Oi, muchachos!', the male passengers were called down to help push the bus back on to the road.

The next day we were too fatigued by the journey and the memory of Welsh teas to do more than investigate the quiet town of Esquel, but the day after that, a Friday, we spent walking off *torta negra* in the national park of Los Alerces, in the foothills of the Andes. Our plane back to Buenos Aires was leaving on Sunday morning from Bariloche, nearly a hundred miles away in northern

Patagonia. Before making our way there, we wanted to visit Cholila, where Butch Cassidy and the Sundance Kid had lived for four years, after fleeing America and the determined detectives of the Pinkerton Agency.

Our bus arrived in Cholila after dusk, but even in the murky half-light we could see that this was not so much a town as a settlement, thrown up to provide scant housing for the workers employed by the enormous Patagonian ranches all around. It was satisfying to see the local men conforming so closely to the gaucho stereotype, in both dress and taciturnity. Some of them swaggered up and down the only street in their traditional pleated bombacha trousers and sombreros, looking threatening in a bow-legged sort of way. We dropped into one bar, to ask for directions to the local hostel, and the drinkers' heads really did swivel to look at us, with a scowling synchronicity they might have learned from spaghetti westerns. It was possible to believe that things had not changed much in Cholila since Butch Cassidy and the Sundance Kid had first ridden into town.

That was in 1901, a year after they and other members of the Wild Bunch had carried out the notorious robbery of the First National Bank at Winnemucca, Nevada. The gang's five leaders had made the endearing but fatal gesture of sending a portrait photograph of themselves to the bank manager. All too soon this vital piece of evidence came to rest at the Pinkerton Detective Agency, which had long had Butch and Sundance at the top of its wanted list.

In his book *In Patagonia*, Bruce Chatwin described Butch Cassidy as intelligent and sensitive, with an interest in British medieval history, particularly Scottish clans. His strong, if unconventional, moral code permitted robbing banks, rustling cattle and redistributing wealth a bit, Robin Hood style. But he would not kill a man and evidently he found it hard to stomach the murderousness of some of his colleagues, including Sundance. Actually, he was anything but butch.

He had left his Mormon home at nineteen, aching for the wide horizons and lawlessness of the Wild West, and before long he had become one of the most wanted outlaws in America, but also one of the most respected. After he served an early spell in prison for dealing in stolen horses, the Wyoming authorities pleaded with Cassidy not to rob again. He could not truthfully promise such a thing, though he did undertake not to rob any more banks in Wyoming. By 1900, the Wild Bunch had robbed five trains, three banks and nine payrolls.

It was fun for a while but, by the end of the century, the police were closing the gap and the West was not as wild as it used to be. Patagonia, where the landscape was similar and the cops slower, seemed like an excellent alternative. In 1901, Butch Cassidy met the Sundance Kid and Etta Place in New York. They spent a week going to operas and the theatre, buying a gold watch for Etta at Tiffany's, before setting sail for Argentina. In Buenos Aires they bought 12,000 acres of Patagonian land and came west to Cholila.

One of Cholila's synchronised drinkers, a huge rough-handed man mashing a toothpick, agreed to taxi us to the hostel, which was a couple of miles out of town. It was run by a German couple, just too young to arouse suspicion, though Patagonia was a favoured haunt of ex-Nazis. After the Second World War, Argentina had proved a popular destination for both Jews and Nazis, but, since the Jews had ended up in Buenos Aires and the Nazis in Patagonia, they were still worlds apart.

I guessed our host might have an obsessional nature, since completed 1,000-piece jigsaws hung on most of the walls – the compiling of jigsaws was evidently an important pastime in Patagonia – but his wife's cooking was the best we had tasted in Argentina: we ate heartily and slept late. The next morning, after a large breakfast, we enquired about transport from Cholila. Our plan was to see Butch Cassidy's house, then take a bus to Bariloche, spending the night there before flying back to Buenos Aires the next morning.

Our German host shook his head sadly at the mention of a bus. 'There's no bus from Cholila today or tomorrow,' he said. 'It's a weekend, you see.' Though the news was a significant blow to us, our host appeared not to be concerned. 'You have to walk to the asphalt road over the hills and see if you can catch a bus there. It's about thirty miles, so you might make it before sunset.'

Then even this brief candle of hope was snuffed out: 'But I don't zink zo.'

The prospect of walking thirty miles with luggage, over hills and in the sun, was not at all attractive, but if we wanted to make the flight we had no choice. I suggested that we might thumb a lift but, with a pessimism I was beginning to feel must be characteristic, the hosteler doubted this would be possible: he said there was 'little movement' in Cholila on a weekend.

There was some truth to his prediction – when we got into town we found that there were people moving around it, but they were moving slowly, with the bow-legged discomfort of men who cannot walk or think straight when not on a horse. The people we asked about Butch Cassidy certainly knew of him, in fact they spoke as if he were still around. 'Boots' house is a little ways along the road,' they kept saying, but when we asked how long a little ways it actually was, they scratched their heads and looked perplexed. Unfortunately no one was available to give us a lift.

Butch Cassidy spent the first winter alone in Cholila, building a cabin at the foot of the mountains for the three of them. In August 1902, he wrote to the mother of an imprisoned outlaw friend:

> I visited the best cities and best parts of South America till I got here. And this part of the country looked so good that I located, and I think for good, for I like the place better every day. I have 300 cattle, 1,500 sheep, and 28 good saddle horses, two men to do my work, also a good four-room house, warehouse, stable, chicken house and some chickens. The only thing lacking is a cook, for I am living in Single Cussedness and sometimes I feel very lonely for I am alone all day and my neighbors don't amount to anything, besides the only language spoken in this country is Spanish, and I don't speak it well enough to converse on the latest scandals so dear to the hearts of all

nations, and without which conversations are very stale, but the country is first class.

More than an hour's walk out of Cholila, when we were beginning to despair of ever reaching the house, let alone the asphalt road or the aeroplane, a pickup slowed down for us to jump on the back. The driver, middle-aged, was accompanied by an older man I took to be his father. They had been shooting, and we shared the ride with a pile of rabbits, bloody and steaming in the cold air.

After about five miles, the driver let us down on the road outside his house, then as we were turning to walk on, his father asked, 'Wait a minute. Are you looking for Boots' house?'

'Yes.'

'Come inside and talk,' said the man. 'My mother knew Boots.'

His name was Américo Villagran and he was sixty, though he looked older, and seemed chastened by the polio-withered leg that must have made him useless as a horseman. He took us into the kitchen, where a young woman was making lunch with a look of put-upon bad humour that was only slightly softened by the present of the rabbits. Reluctantly, she invited us to sit down.

Américo told us that his mother had lived next door to the gringo outlaws when she was a child. 'She often used to go round there and they would entertain her. They used to throw coins up and shoot them in mid-air. Etta was by far the best shot.'

'What were they like?'

'They were very nice people, very friendly and polite. Sometimes they went to the neighbours' parties, but mostly they kept to themselves. No one even knew that they were outlaws until after they left.'

'We should charge for this information,' muttered the young woman at the sink.

The three Americans had not endured Patagonia's quiet life for long. In 1905, they held up a bank in a neighbouring province and, after a second robbery in 1907, they sold the Cholila ranch and vanished, never to be seen there again. No one was sure what had happened to Butch and Sundance after that. The most common belief was that they had crossed the Andes and found a base in Chile from which to make forays into Bolivia. After one massive haul they had died at the hands of the Bolivian police, who had records to this effect. But there were various dissenters from this version, among them a former Bolivian president and amateur sleuth, who used his high office to launch a thorough investigation into their deaths and concluded that they were not, after all, buried in the bleak hill-top cemetery. Like many other Butch and Sundance fans, he preferred to think that they might have returned alive to the United States.

About a mile up the road from Américo's house we spotted a thicket concealing a tumbledown shack. The place looked abandoned, and the field in front of it was scattered with the bones of a cow, picked clean, then sun-blanched over weeks or months. Finding a way through the thicket and into the yard, we peered through dusty windows into the house. Through one, I saw piles of old petticoats – Etta's? – and broken-down furniture. An outhouse was filled with empty liquor bottles. Yet it also looked as if the house had been abandoned that very morning. The stable doors were open; horse dung steamed in the yard and a pungent smell of urine hung in the air. There was a new padlock on the door. Further down the road we had passed three riders in ponchos, slouching on their horses and chewing the requisite toothpicks with a Clintish menace. Perhaps these were the new occupants of the shack; they might also be outlaws.

Butch Cassidy had built this American cabin with his own hands, ninety years ago. Now it was slowly falling down. No tourist body had come to preserve it, there was no shop offering Butch and Sundance T-shirts, no visitor centre or theme park. Once again the outlaws had eluded authority and given themselves up to the landscape. Looking from the empty stable towards the Andes, and Chile beyond them, I could imagine that they had bolted only moments before.

It was a glorious day of sun and blue sky, but little heat. The purple mountain backdrop and the yellow prairie, stretching to the horizon, were perfect. Everything was as it should be. I felt a pure exhilaration, as I turned away from Butch Cassidy's house and looked towards the hills to the east. There were fewer than twenty miles now, between us and the asphalt road, and still about six hours before sunset. We started walking.

CHAPTER NINE

Call This a Democracy?

'MAYBE I'M PARANOID, but I think people are frightened,' said Julia. 'There's a feeling that we don't know what's going on in the country. Some of my friends have started getting death-threats, just like the old days.'

Back in Buenos Aires, I was sitting in a tango hall with Raquel and half a dozen female psychoanalysts who were friends of hers. I had recently joined the group for tango lessons, which was a mistake because they analysed every step, and even tried to reform those steps they disliked, which infuriated the men who partnered us. There was an understanding among tango aficionados that it was charitable for an old-timer to invite a beginner to dance, and several elderly men came to this weekly session precisely to offer us that charity. In wrinkled grey suits and with outsized noses and ears, they were like a small herd of elephants treading carefully on the dance-floor.

The *tangueros* were affable enough, but my friends' awkward behaviour had wounded them, so now we spent most of our time sitting around a table, waiting to be asked to dance, and complaining that it was very sexist, this having to wait, and that tango itself was very macho, that Argentine men were macho, and that *everything* was wrong with Argentine men, *everything* wrong with Argentina. While we were analysing everything, we learned nothing about the tango.

'At least when there was a dictator it was easy to identify the enemy,' said Fabiana, who was the only Freudian, that night, among Lacanians. 'Now there are various organisations, accumulating tremendous power, who aren't answerable to anyone.'

'Business mafias,' said Raquel.

'Exactly. And all the one-time torturers have been recycled as security guards or bully-boys. Old habits die hard. They're the guys making the death-threats.'

'The corruption in this country is shameless,' cried Julia. 'The poor are getting poorer, and the rich isolate themselves in private estates, with armed guards on the gates.'

'I think there's something wrong with the national character,' said Raquel. 'What we need is good, cold weather. People in the north don't have these problems.'

'We should all move to Norway,' said Julia.

'That's right, we should all move north.'

The other psychoanalysts sitting around the table laughed their agreement. 'Or south?' someone suggested. 'What about Patagonia?'

And yet many things in Argentina were improving. The telephones worked much better now and the operators had a sweet American habit of introducing themselves and asking how they might help. For the first time in Argentina's history, tax evasion was a fool's game and, in spite of the hisses that accompanied its advertisements in cinemas, the Inland Revenue was reporting record returns. The pavements had improved, and the Paraguayans had disappeared from our avenue, closing behind them the pits that had been such a useful aid to looking up skirts – then again, the skirts were longer now, so perhaps it was time for them to move on.

Most importantly, the 'wall of silence' that separated Argentina from its past was starting to show cracks. Recently, an ex-naval officer Adolfo Scilingo had confessed to throwing the drugged bodies of young men and women out of planes during night flights over the River Plata. As the first official confirmation of something that had long been known, the revelation caused a painful catharsis in the nation. The language Scilingo used to describe the experience of sending others to their death was chilling: it was a kind of 'communion', he said. The army chaplain employed to soothe the officers' consciences had told them the executions were necessary and 'humane'. President Menem, displeased by the revelations, tried to discredit Scilingo, but already a process of truth-telling was under way. Soon afterwards, the commander-in-chief of the army, Colonel Martín Balza, apologised for 'excesses' committed by the military during the Dirty War. Then, a conventional wisdom, that Argentines were not interested in the past, was toppled when a new poll showed that more than half of respondents wanted to know the truth of what had happened. 'We won't be a mature country until we face up to the Dirty War,' wrote one commentator.

The ending of compulsory military service was perhaps the most important step in breaking the fatal dichotomy of dictatorship and rebellion that had dogged Argentina throughout its history.

'I feel as if we're no longer sleepwalking,' said Martín. 'We don't like this president, but instead of taking to the streets we'll wait for elections and vote him out. We're breaking the cycle of reaction.'

The militant activism of previous years was barely a memory. A poll carried out among teenagers revealed that very few of them knew who Che Guevara was (most of them thought he might have been a tango singer). Even the graffiti was more to do with sex and pop these days, and less to do with politics – but there was still the expectation that Evita would return, there was still a belief that one day the torturers would be punished.

Would they?

One very hot morning I went to meet a military expert for a 'working' breakfast to discuss the evolution of the Argentine army in recent times. I knew that Carlos had occupied a high position in the invasion of the Falkland Islands, and also that he was a great admirer of the British forces. I had heard that he was a charming man, with a great sense of humour. As far as the army was concerned, I assumed that he was moderate, a moderniser.

Thanks to some confusion about the rendezvous, which had me waiting for ten minutes in a café on the opposite corner, I was late and flustered when I arrived at Carlos' table. He had joked on the telephone that I would recognise him by his big head, and he was right: it was almost as big as the hairdresser's head I had seen floating wanly at the morgue. Indeed, it was the only way to distinguish him from the dozens of men in suits sitting alone at rows of tables, starting the day with newspapers and a shot of caffeine.

Here he was, this big-headed man, laughing and good-natured about the delay, embracing me with a warmth I found surprising but appealing. We ordered coffees and he began to tell me of his great admiration and love of Britain and of British figures, such as Churchill, about whom he read everything he could lay his hands on. He told me that he spoke fluent English – and he demonstrated this by dropping words and phrases into our conversation – having received most of his education from three English governesses. The memory of these 'lovable spinsters', the daughters of railway engineers, caused him to weep briefly. 'Forgive me,' he said, removing the tears with a hand that was surprisingly small in relation to his head, 'but I loved them so much.' Indeed, he spoke often of love, even going so far as to say that it was 'pure affection' for Britain that had made him determined to fight in the Falklands – and his experience of the war had only increased his admiration. He felt that the leaders of the British forces had, in a short time, realised something 'crucial' about Argentines.

'That is that we aren't war dogs. We have a great capacity to improvise, we're very creative – Maradona's a perfect example – but we leave everything to the last moment. Our attitude is: if you want to get an A at school you have to work hard, but you can get by with a C. We can attack, because it is about going forward, but defence is psychologically much harder and that is where we fail.'

Carlos had a strategist's habit of making tiny notes on the back of paper napkins as he spoke, miniature plans with dates on them and key words, sometimes underlined. I found his manner and appearance engaging. He looked like a gentle man, perhaps a bumbler. His face was made of rubbery folds that creased and eased like a concertina to accommodate the extent of his expressions. Much of the time he wore a grin so wide that it demanded several folds of flesh at either end, and he was prone to hoot with laughter, though he could also be instantly grave or emotional, for example when remembering favourite governesses and generals.

Carlos liked talking; in fact it quickly became apparent that he could talk and talk, without any intervention from me. Many of his observations began, 'If you're asking...', but I rarely was. Rather, Carlos posed his own questions and answered them. He deliberated, expounded, reminisced, made notes. He described with emotion a childhood that had been buried in military history books, bent on soldiering. The memory of his mother, who had nagged him to study, threatened to provoke more tears.

'Did the army live up to your expectations?' I asked, and I saw the pen quiver, uncertain, over its note-making. It was a moment I had anticipated, and I expected him now to talk about the failures of the military, its history of wrong-headed interventions in politics, their disastrous culmination in the *proceso*.

Carlos hesitated. He said, very carefully: 'My wife always complains that I love the army more than her, and I always say I don't – but the truth is probably that I do. I've spent the best years of my life in the army, with very great friends.' The concertina smile eased outwards. 'We used to call ourselves "the same old bastards", because whenever there were difficult jobs to be done, it was always us lot, always the same old bastards, who ended up being asked to do it.' He let the smile reach its full extent, then roared with laughter in a contagious way that had me laughing too, although I was far from appreciating the army spirit, and I wondered what he meant by 'difficult jobs'.

'We first worked together in the 1960s,' Carlos went on, 'when Che Guevara turned up in Bolivia. At that time the number of officers technically prepared for combat was very small. They got together twenty instructors and sent us to the jungle to teach people how to fight guerillas in jungle areas.'

As he went on to describe the relative difficulties of urban and rural combat, the problems posed by venomous snakes and the lack of water, I became aware of a physical discomfort, unlocated, but something like a feather drawn across the inside surfaces of my body. Talking on, Carlos mentioned that he had been lucky to receive training from North Americans in Panama. 'By the end of the 1960s we had all come to realise, for different reasons, that we were going to have to fight guerillas,' he said, casually.

It was then, with a thudding of the heart, that I realised Carlos was an 'ex-repressor'. This charming man with the concertina-smile was one of the *asesinos* the graffiti spoke about. He had killed people, perhaps he had tortured them. Panic quickened my blood.

'What did you make of Colonel Balza's apology?' I asked, as a way to investigate his hindsight. He might condone the harsh measures taken against the guerillas, but surely he deplored the persecution of innocents.

'I thought it was wrong,' he said simply.

Carlos was not repentant, then, and that changed everything around this table as swiftly as a new camera angle brought to bear on a familiar scene. The way we talked was necessarily different: there was a tension, a menace, to the exchange. Even the quality of noise, of light around us seemed to alter perceptibly. My tape-machine was the vital axis of this changed scene; I was aware of a need to extract information and to make sure that it was registered.

'Did you know what was going on from the start?' I heard my voice sounding young and naive. I was still giving Carlos chances to distance himself from the worst of it.

Unsmiling, he would not take them. He blinked with deliberation, fixing his eyes on mine.

'I would be disrespecting you if I lied. Yes, I knew what was going on. And if you're asking me, was I obliged to fight the subversives,

the answer is no. Not only was I *not* obliged to do that, but most of
the time I went on missions *because I felt like it.*'

There was no trace of the bumbler now, the man who had wept
for his governesses. Carlos spoke fluently and the stream of words
was, perhaps deliberately, disarming. Yet many of the observations
led into labyrinths. I had the impression that memories and images
assailed him and that he was trying, even now, to make sense of their
meaning. At times he seemed oblivious to my presence.

'In October 1976 we were returning from a really revolting,
sickening operation in Buenos Aires' – he said 'sickening' in
English – 'everyone in the car was disgusted, silent. I remember
thinking then that the point of all wars was to reach a peace. Both
sides want *their* brand of peace, but a peace nonetheless. But how
were we going to achieve it? The war had been going on for seven
months by then and my wife said I had aged ten years. It was a
terrible, terrible, frightful time.'

'Was there no other way to suppress the guerillas?' There was the
silly girl's voice again.

'That's a good question.' He seemed to consider this quite carefully, as if we were talking of a football match, not of many thousands
of deaths. 'In retrospect there's always a better way. Perhaps World
War Two need not have ended with the atomic bomb. Look' – he
moved the coffee cups and leaned on the table – 'I'll tell you an
anecdote. In 1973, a few days after the coup in Chile the Montoneros
held a big anti-Pinochet demonstration in Buenos Aires. One
evening, coming back from the military school, two colleagues and
I decided to go and watch the march. We parked the Citroën on a
street corner and watched the demonstrators as they filed by, thousands and thousands of Montoneros, some of them with their faces
covered. I remember that my colleague said, "You know, we're
going to have to kill these guys, otherwise they'll kill us." My other
friend, a quiet bloke with a nice wife, said – and I've never forgotten
this – he said: "What a bummer that we have to kill them, because
they're Argentine, just like us."'

There was the crease of a sad smile then. 'You know what went wrong in the 1970s? A failure of tolerance – on both sides.'

I could not hold his eye, nor could I think of anything to say. I felt my mouth dry, wordless. My linguistic skills evaporated. The vocabulary, the grammar, the nuance turned to nothing, like sliding cherries on a fruit-machine: blank, blank, blank.

'Excuse me a moment,' I said. Carlos nodded and picked up his mobile telephone. The only woman in the café, I felt as if I drew every male glance on the way to the lavatory, every one of them suspicious. Could they all be ex-repressors? I took my time in the sanctuary of the cubicle, and then I stood a while before the mirror, examining my face briefly for signs of change. I associated these revelations of murder, of torture, with an inevitable ageing. Even if it were not visible, there ought to be some internal damage, some wrinkling of the heart or the soul. How could one not be injured by an encounter such as this? Carlos' wife said he had aged ten years in seven months of bloodshed. Running water over my wrists to cool my blood, I told myself, 'I'll just get through this, and the rest of the day is mine.' I would go shopping or sit in the park, I would rediscover life's normality in small things.

Back at the table, Carlos said: 'You ask me if it could not have been any other way. You might just as well ask, could Argentine history have been different? I know one thing: people who are very interested in the past have no interest in the present or the future. No one can drive a car at 150 kilometres an hour looking backwards. You have to focus all your senses forward.'

'At least, I suppose' – I fumbled for words – 'it could never happen again, could it?'

For the first time in over an hour, Carlos roared with the familiar laughter I had liked when first we sat down. But now the laughter meant something so different, it was horrifying. 'Oh please,' he said, 'this is Latin America. This is Latin America. You're talking about trying to change human nature.'

'You mean Latin Americans are peculiarly cut out for violence?'

'I don't know,' said Carlos, and he added, '*I'm not so sure.*' The fact that he chose to say them in English made the words ominous, as if he were sharing the violence with me, insinuating it into my territory. 'The Northern Irish situation doesn't bode well.'

At the end of the interview, a neat pile of annotated paper napkins lay on the table between us. As we prepared to leave, Carlos picked up the pile and tore it into tiny pieces which he sprinkled into the ashtray.

'There's one thing that gives me great hope,' he said, by way of a conclusion. 'If you read books about us from the last century, you see that Argentines haven't really changed, in spite of the millions of immigrants who came here. That must mean that identity isn't only transmitted through people but through the earth itself. I am comforted by that idea.'

Yet it seemed an appalling idea to me, for I suddenly had an image of a land soaked in blood, like the slaughter-ground described by Hudson with its 'old and ever-newly moistened crust of dust and coagulated blood'. What Carlos said implied that nothing would ever change in Argentina, because everyone was born out of the same bloody soil. I had an impression, too, that he wanted nothing to change.

I left the café feeling sick – and both surprised and satisfied by that reaction: it was interesting to know that an encounter like mine with Carlos could turn the stomach in real life, and not just in thrillers. The nausea, which in other circumstances might constitute a betrayal, came here as a reassurance. It meant that I had, bodily, rejected Carlos' defence of the Dirty War. That was a relief because I knew that my emotional reaction had been more ambivalent. There had been an urge to believe the rubbery face that laughed and wept so easily.

They had been two intense hours, I had eaten nothing and the mid-morning heat was oppressive. As I walked along beside the gardens towards the National Library, an overdose of caffeine prickled in my veins. I tried to analyse the nature of my shock: I had spoken to someone who had been a killer and might have been a torturer – that was hardly unusual in Argentina, there were hundreds of them around. Yet it occurred to me that I was not shaken so much by the revelations Carlos had made as by the way in which my first impression of him had been so wrong. I might have come dangerously close to accepting that what he said was true, that 'there was no other way'. Friends had told me of similar experiences. 'Whenever you meet repressors they are charming,' Uki Goñi had said, 'whereas the ex-guerillas are unpleasant. They seem to have no body language. They give nothing away.'

I walked on, past the square where a giant statue of Evita was once to have been erected. The woman who wanted for herself only a footnote in the history books had opted, in the end, for something grander. The model she approved was almost the size of the Statue of Liberty, and Evita, the great nationalist, who had an American surgeon, whose embalmer and biographer were Spaniards, chose an Italian to make it. But, like so much else, Evita's monument fell victim to a change of regime. At least she still had a bust at the Children's Republic.

In the parkland that skirted the main road, clusters of people were practising the deliberate art of t'ai chi, folding their limbs like origami into new shapes, in hope of releasing a new tranquillity. It was the latest fashionable way to fight urban stress. Under a chestnut tree, a dog-walker floundered as his canine charges made a maypole of him. Finally he freed himself by freeing them, and one by one the dogs bounded across the grass, a greyhound trailing labrador, retriever, spaniel down to the smallest terrier. It was not true that the first would be last and the last, first. The first were always first because they were stronger. A young woman who was sunbathing under the statue of San Martín reached instinctively for her shirt as she saw the dogs rounding on her with their drooling tongues.

I climbed the hill towards the Recoleta cemetery with the thought of going to talk to Hugo about what had happened, but he would not yet be at work, so instead I crossed to the strip of smart bars on the other side of the road. The terrace of La Biela café was already full of wealthy divorcees, reflecting one another in their sunglasses and exchanges of *angustia*. Should I stop here for a coffee – yet *more* coffee? I felt too unsettled to be at home; I wanted to be some time in the streets, because I felt that the morning's encounter had changed my relationship with the city. I was more complicit, now, in the bloody tangle that bound *porteños* together. I would take a long route back to the flat, stopping off in one or two of my favourite bookshops. I knew nowhere in the world where the bookshops and cafés were more inviting. Perhaps there was no city where the atmosphere in the streets was more intoxicating.

'I know Buenos Aires well,' I thought. 'My friends are here; it could be my home. I love it and I hate it. I can't live here, but, wherever else I live, I'll always feel the lack of it.'

Five blocks from home I began to feel dizzy and even drunk, as though my head was filling with air. It was not an unpleasant sensation, but it made the walk arduous. I turned my head to the right and the street on my left swung away from me and, as I crossed the road, the cars seemed to be rushing at me. Was it the combination of heat and humidity that made people feel so strange in Buenos Aires, or the famous 'low pressure'? Raquel, vociferous enemy of the weather, ate salt sprinkled on bread and butter to counter its worst effects. She would have told me that I was foolish to walk such a long way on an empty stomach in this heat. Heeding her imagined scolding, I stopped at a kiosk and bought a biscuit, then joined a row of old women sitting on a bench to eat it. It was comforting, in the circumstances, to eavesdrop on their familiar talk of illnesses and pills.

'She would be nearly eighty now,' the old woman next to me said presently, indicating the posters of Evita stuck on to a wall opposite. The remark was really for her friend, but she turned to include me, as an equal occupant of the bench, in her observations. 'I can't think of her as anything but young, it's funny that, isn't it? I am growing old, but Evita will always be young.'

It was a picture I had not seen before, of a very young woman with loose, curly hair, laughing. The face, containing no rancour, was beautiful.

'She looks very happy in that picture,' I said. 'I'm not used to seeing her so happy.'

'Well, that was long before everything, dear,' said my companion with a woman's gift for generalisation. 'Where are you from, dear?'

'I'm from Britain,' I said, and two faces loomed on the other side of my neighbour.

'How's Princess Diana, then?' one asked.

'Not too happy at the moment, I should imagine.'

'What about the London smog?' said the other.

'They cleaned up the smog in the 1950s,' I confessed, with a feeling that I had finally got something off my chest. 'It's much better now, though of course the traffic pollution is worse.' I thought I ought to add that, because I could see that the old ladies were disappointed about the smog. It was one of the most enduring images of England; Argentines liked imagining stern, moustachioed men in bowler hats peering at one another through an industrial fug. Perhaps it made them feel superior. 'The English presumed to rule the world,' they might think, 'but we know that they're blind at home.'

When I got home, I stopped off to see Raquel, who was having her hair done in the kitchen. 'You look absolutely white!' she exclaimed and I told her about the morning's meeting with Carlos, and about my doubts concerning his part in *el proceso*.

'Of course he tortured people!' Raquel said and she and the hairdresser both laughed delightedly at my naivety. 'What did you expect?'

For ages, I put off listening to my interview with Carlos then, when I did, I found that a strange thing had happened to the recording. It may have been that the cassette or the batteries were damaged by heat, age or both. Whatever the reason, the result was that parts of our conversation were speeded up and other parts played very slow. Sometimes my nervous questions sounded like the insignificant chirping of a bird, and at other times they borrowed a masculine authority, while Carlos alternated between Disney pig and automaton, neither version easily intelligible. The darkest of the observations he had made in the café were now lent a Frankenstein monstrosity on the tape. 'Ter-ri-ble,' droned the voice. 'Ter-ri-ble years.'

It was hot again, so much hotter than I had remembered was possible. The ants paraded back into the kitchen, triumphant as Irish marchers. Mysterious creatures began to multiply once more in the bathroom drain. I squirted everything I could find that was lethal down the drain and, when that did no good, I tipped in a whole bottle of Eau de something I had been given at one of Martín's launch parties. It smelled fatal, yet the creatures thrived on it.

The battle between heat and water recommenced. By day, the temperature soared. At night there were massive, frightening thunderstorms. A series of holes in the roof admitted xylophonic drips. A routine had been established, now, by which we telephoned the administrator to complain about the leaks and, once the complaints had mounted to a certain level, he sent round someone to look at the roof and to make a diagnosis. Nothing was done about it. The complaints mounted again, someone came round again, nothing was done again. I still regularly woke up with a wet face.

The statistics concerning rats, accidents and pollution continued to appal, but there was some good news on cockroaches: I read in a magazine that only three of a possible three thousand varieties existed in Argentina. The bad news was that a large member of one of these families was crawling up my sitting-room wall. My friend Guillermo and I followed the beast's progress as it moved steadily towards the ceiling and then, at the level of the sleeping area, paused. The cockroach waved its antennae briefly, receiving untold information from the atmosphere. It began to open, then resettled its wings.

'It's one of those ones that can fly,' said Guillermo, disconcertingly.

'Which means it's probably going to fly into my hair.'

'I could kill it for you,' he offered.

Guillermo had come to say goodbye, because he was leaving Buenos Aires. After years of working two full-time jobs and being underpaid for both, he had decided to join his girlfriend in Chile, where the economic prospects were brighter.

We watched the cockroach in its crucial moment of decision-making. Would it carry on upwards towards the rafters, or return to the murky shade of the skirting board?

'What will you miss most about Argentina?' I asked.

'Pizza, tango, Maradona.'

'Maradona? Even now?'

'He's still a maestro.'

The suspension of Diego Maradona from the 1994 World Cup, after traces of ephedrine, a banned drug, were found in his urine, had been met with a terrible anguish in Buenos Aires. Some thought it the worst disgrace ever to befall the country, a humiliation equal to Argentina's defeat in the Falklands.

Maradona was the nation's greatest hero. Like Carlos Gardel and Eva Perón, he had been born in poverty and risen young to the status of icon. His opinion was solicited on every subject, from democratic reform to Papal encyclicals. The words 'Thanks, Diego' were often to be seen humbly inscribed on suburban walls, alongside the more affirmative 'Evita lives'. His talent was always described in religious terms. To Argentines he was a 'Messiah', a 'God'.

Maradona's fall, when it came, was equally biblical. As the news of his suspension spread, Buenos Aires plunged itself into mourning, hundreds of fans gathering in tearful solidarity around the Obelisk, the capital's most virile monument. Many of the cafés that had installed television sets before the World Cup, covered them in black shrouds. Confined to his hotel room, Maradona was shown howling 'They have cut off my legs!' There was a rumour that soccer-mad President Menem might intervene to save the player's reputation.

A poll taken at the time suggested that half of all Argentines thought that Maradona had been the victim of an international plot and later a thriller was published, *Innocent*, about an Argentine footballer who fell foul of a CIA conspiracy to discredit him and his country. The ephedrine was cunningly administered to the novel's hero in his communion wine before a match. *Innocent* was publicised with a poster campaign declaring, 'This isn't the Bible, but it is about God.'

I had met Julio Llinás, who wrote *Innocent*. He was a quiet, reclusive man, a product of Argentina's landed classes, fallen on hard times. Over supper, we talked about Che Guevara, who had gone out briefly with Julio's cousin and whom he had found intriguing. But Julio had little interest in football or Maradona. He had written *Innocent* as a money-spinner to support more serious writing. 'It was entirely fictitious, but now Maradona's going around saying it could really have happened. Well, if it suits him to say so, that's his business.'

Maradona's pride and career had been injured, but it was good to know that his *viveza criolla* survived intact.

'It *is* going towards your bed,' warned Guillermo, when I returned from the kitchen with more wine.

The cockroach had reached the balcony and we watched it climb over the iron balustrade and on to the bedside table. It made a clumsy negotiation of the collection of pots and trinkets on the table's surface. Then, showing a high-wire daring not usually associated with cockroaches, it launched itself on to the lamp cord that dangled between table and bed and began to make a tricky descent towards the mattress.

'What about you? What are you going to miss?' asked Guillermo.

'I'll miss the tango halls and cafés, the way people go to eat out at midnight. I'll miss friends.'

The cockroach reached the point where the cord touched the bed, and now it made a smooth transfer to the mattress. We watched, horrified, as the brown oval disappeared under the sheets.

'I won't miss the cockroaches.'

I had decided, finally, to take Máximo's advice: I would flee Buenos Aires. In the end, there was no choice but for me to leave, even though it meant leaving alone, and with no clear idea of where I was going. It was not just that I was unhappy, the unhappiness had gained a quarter in me, it had become something that I cherished and relied on. Every day I woke up with a feeling of resignation; the face that I saw in the mirror made no demands on the day.

The oppressors had gone, but Buenos Aires oppressed me all the same. Wandering its streets, I seemed to feel the pain of history underfoot. Every street and square bore the memory of an atrocity, a promise unfulfilled. There were the cafés on Avenida Corrientes from which students had 'disappeared'. There were the torture centres with their elegant European façades. There was the Plaza de Mayo, where Evita had bayed for the blood of the Oligarchy. 'If it is necessary, we shall execute justice with our own hands.' I stood in queues at the supermarket, watching blood dripping from the trolley ahead, and felt defeated.

'We must never be complacent,' said a voice on the radio. 'We must never think that the past is over and done with. There is danger around every corner. We must never say "What happened here could not happen again." It could happen, unless we are all vigilant.'

One afternoon, in a café, I noticed a woman sitting at a neighbouring table with two friends. She was young and pretty, but it was her voice, straining to control an overburdening emotion, that captured my attention. 'I just can't see a way out any more,' the woman said. 'I feel as if my life is going like this': I watched her place a finger on the table-top and draw a steep downward curve. Looking up, I caught her expression at the moment it gave way to tears. Mine was a heartfelt empathy: I had an inkling that my life was going the same way.

The last interview I did in Buenos Aires was with Eugenia de Chikoff, Argentina's 'queen of etiquette'. Following in the footsteps of her illustrious Russian father, Count de Chikoff, Eugenia had been grooming image-conscious *porteños* for forty years. She had prepared presidents and supermodels, senators, judges and professionals, young brides-to-be. The cream of Buenos Aires society came here to learn European etiquette in a course of twelve lessons which started with the correct use of cutlery and progressed to the delicate art of conversation. I had wanted to meet her for two years. Three days before I left, I finally got through to her on the telephone.

'I am alone and I have no way of vetting the people who come to see me,' she said, as she greeted me at the door. She was fair and deceptively youthful. 'But there are secret police living in this building, and that makes me feel better.' I stepped into the small airless apartment she referred to as her 'school', reflecting that the same knowledge would have made many Argentines feel worse.

We sat down and Eugenia, elegantly dressed in Chinese silk, explained her technique for teaching manners. 'There must never be talk of politics, race, death, religion or illness at table,' she explained. 'But, depending on your degree of intelligence, you may talk of reincarnation, philosophy or travel, all of them succulent topics.'

I wanted to know about Eva Perón, who had been sent to study etiquette with the Chikoffs, when her husband grew tired of watching her eat out of tins.

'My father met General Perón at the military school where he gave classes and the General asked him to teach Evita,' Eugenia said, and she permitted herself a discreet smile. 'He explained that she made a slurping noise when she ate soup.'

'Did the Count manage to show her how to eat it properly?'

'Oh yes. She turned out to be my father's best pupil. After her state visit to Europe, we got hundreds of letters commenting on her marvellous manners. Evita was not really a republican, you know, but an authentic aristocrat. She was a queen. At home we held her in very high esteem and great affection.'

'It must have been difficult to keep Evita off the question of politics at the dinner table.'

'She had a tendency to use seismic words which was problematic,' Eugenia admitted. 'All the rancour she felt against the upper classes rushed out of her. She couldn't contain it.'

'Do you think she was partly responsible for Argentina's current problems?'

'It is not permitted to speak of politics here,' said Eugenia firmly. 'Why not ask me about the glorious landscape in the south of Argentina, or the great waterfall at Iguazu? Why not ask me about the indigenous cultures of Salta and Jujuy? Please, do not ask me to lower myself by criticising my country.'

I beat a quick retreat to the sanctuary of etiquette. 'How good are Argentine manners nowadays?' I asked.

'Sometimes I feel very depressed when I see the graffiti,' said Eugenia. 'You know, the young are avid for guidance. Once mothers were monsters who knew how to inculcate discipline in their off-spring; unfortunately that is no longer the case.'

Eugenia told me that one of the worst things to have happened in the history of manners was the rise of the individual. 'You can trace it back to Napoleon and the beginning of the French Republic, a terrible time when the aristocracy and the monarchy were destroyed. Poor King Louis and Marie-Antoinette lost their heads.' She spoke with horror, as if these were quite recent events, and I remembered that Count de Chikoff had come to Argentina fleeing the Russian Revolution. He had been one of the more successful immigrants – there was even a tango written about him.

'So you believe that self-love and egotism date from that time?'

'What do self-love and egotism have to do with what I am telling you?'

'Well, I thought you were lamenting the rise of individualism.'

'You have misunderstood!' cried Eugenia. 'I was speaking of *individuales*, individual place-mats! Les napperons, comprenez-vous? Perhaps you have not seen this phenomenon so much in Britain – I am sure that the Queen allows only tablecloths at Buckingham Palace, but it is a terrible problem here, and also in North America. Napoleon started it by tearing up the tablecloth. He tore up civility at the same time.'

'Oh, I *see*,' I said, though really I did not.

'Miriam,' she said, and it was the second time she had mistaken my name, 'you must never shake or nod your head. Remember that you wear a metaphysical crown. The jewels in your crown are youth, beauty, intelligence and daring. But when you move your head the crown tumbles to the floor.' She used an elegant hand to describe this catastrophic movement. 'Imagine what would happen if the Queen of England were to do the same, with all those kilos she has to carry on her head.'

'I'm sorry. I'll try to remember.' I saw now that Señorita de Chikoff was indeed motionless: her head erect, her legs uncrossed, her hands laid daintily in her lap.

'I'm sure that you won't forget from now on. Whenever you start to move your head, you'll remember me.'

When the interview was finished, Eugenia went to find me a copy of her book on etiquette. While I waited, she suggested that I read about my star sign in a book on the zodiac. The book said I was adventurous, flighty and liable to betray friends and lovers. It advised that I might find suitable employment as a philosopher, travel agent, writer or, strangely – considering my obvious lack of moral fibre – as a nun.

I made to say goodbye to Eugenia at the door of her apartment, but she tutted at me. 'Always see your guest as far as the lift, Melinda,' she said, 'and call the lift for them.'

When the lift arrived she kissed me goodbye. 'Bon voyage!' she called, and as the lift took me down I thought I heard her cry: 'Take care never to lose your crown!' I opened the book she had given me, and saw that it was made out to a 'traveller from afar'.

CHAPTER TEN

Going Home

'I T'S MY FIRST time,' the woman in the aisle seat said.

I had guessed as much when squeezing past her bony knees to claim my place by the window. Although she was small, the woman filled her seat with an anxious solidity that marked her out as a first-timer. Her body-language was wrong; she had not learned the traveller's tricks of accommodation.

In an effort to contain so much anxiety, perhaps, an air hostess had tucked the woman into a tartan travel-rug and buckled the seat-belt over it, even though there were still twenty minutes until take-off. She was severely confined, yet I felt sure that the woman had accepted this imprisonment without demur: she looked like someone to whom things were done, not one of life's doers.

'There's really no need to worry,' I said, to make amends for the meanness of that thought. I set about reassuring my companion with references to the comparative safety of air travel set against, say, crossing the road or carrying out domestic chores. I smiled into her frightened face in a way I hoped was soothing.

It was a relief finally to be starting the journey home. I had arrived early at the airport, and then the plane was delayed, so for three hours I had sat in the departure lounge watching the escaping aircraft melt in the shimmering heat, while muzak versions of Beatles songs were played too loud over the tannoy.

The last week in Buenos Aires had seemed long and the business of saying goodbye to people almost excruciatingly prolonged. Argentine sentiment balked at the cold ritual of farewells and, although there had been a party, and all the guests were dispatched with embraces and promises to keep in touch, many of them had later telephoned or reappeared to say goodbye again. Even mild acquaintances wanted to take leave of me personally. In the last few days, I had found myself bidding fond farewells to the hairdresser, the baker, a couple of librarians and the staff of various local cafés.

When I went to say goodbye to the newsagents, Osvaldo told me that he had got another teaching job. He was clearly pleased to have returned to the classroom, much though he enjoyed sparring with passers-by over newspapers.

'In the first lesson I ask the children what studying history's good for,' he said. 'They usually say "nothing". Then I tell them about the dictatorship, and I ask them if their parents think dictatorship is a good thing. They mostly say "no". So I show them that history does have a purpose. It *is* possible to change things, to make sure mistakes aren't repeated.'

When not engaged in goodbyes, I spent my last days in Buenos Aires doing the rounds of favourite bookshops, cafés and ice-cream parlours. I lingered on street corners, trying to capture in my mind's eye the urban angles of buildings and rooftops that photographs could never properly convey.

The American playwright Eugene O'Neil, who had arrived in Buenos Aires as a 'gentleman' in 1907 and was reduced to destitution in just two years, wrote that there was no bench he had not slept on in the capital. I collected benches too: I sat where O'Neil had slept, watching the city move through its day from different vantage points. I saw the women clattering to work on their high heels. At mid-day, the parks and squares were scattered with the bodies of men, sprawled like corpses where heat had felled them. Outside Congress, I watched children cooling off in the water around the monument, which now wore a new skin of graffiti. 'If this is democracy,' cried the black ink, 'what the hell was dictatorship?'

'I feel like an old man in a Third World country,' Pablo said, when I went to bid a third and final goodbye to him and Raquel. They had recently returned from a month's holiday in Florida. It was Pablo's first trip abroad for twenty-five years and he was taken aback by the efficiency and civility of the Americans. The harsh truth of how those years had been wasted in Argentina had suddenly been brought to bear on him. Pablo described the holiday as the experience of stepping out of a cave into sunlight, only to have to go back into the cave again. It was enough to make anyone feel old.

'But why a Third World country? Isn't it bad to feel old anywhere?'

'No, it's worse here. At least old people in the United States are comfortable. They look relaxed, they go grey, they get fat. Here people's faces are marked by the strain of having to fight all the time.'

'Why don't you go grey and get fat, Pablo? Start a trend.'

'He's too vain,' Raquel said, and we laughed.

'You're *all* too vain,' I pointed out.

Packing, which I had dreaded, had taken no time in the end: the possessions accumulated during my years in Buenos Aires were easily accommodated in two small suitcases, and there was much that I was leaving behind. Most of my clothes would by now have found their way to new owners in the shanty towns. I was taking away books, a few ornaments, pictures and mementoes of my travels across the continent. I had my metaphorical crown, too, though that was always slipping off.

The aeroplane was accelerating towards take-off, and I heard the woman in the aisle seat gasp. Her face was immobile with fear, as if to move any part of it were to jeopardise the aeroplane's equilibrium. One of her knobbled hands fluttered in the air, painting crosses to ward off disaster while the other had delved under the rug to find a crucifix and was clutching it to the tartan ledge of her bosom.

I held my hand out on the empty seat between us. 'Hold on to me if you like,' I said, and the woman immediately locked on to my hand, like a child. Her eyes, tightly closed, issued tears. Her fingers fastened their grip as the plane accelerated down the runway then swung miraculously into the air.

For some minutes, we held hands, like lovers at a funfair, as the aeroplane turned on one wing-tip, offering a panorama of the woodland surrounding the airport. It was a beautiful view – but I knew that the dense canopy of the forest enclosed a dreadful secret: this area had been a killing ground during the Dirty War; murdered men and women had once hung from the branches beneath this verdant foliage.

Only when we had been in the air a good five minutes did the woman release her grip.

'That was the worst bit,' I said. 'You'll enjoy the next fourteen hours, wait and see.'

She nodded, without opening her eyes, and gulped at the rarefied air. 'It's just that it's such a long time,' she murmured.

'Yes, but the time passes quickly. They show films later on, and there are meals. Everyone always says the food is awful, but I like it. It's like being an astronaut or something, eating your food out of boxes. We're lucky to have an extra seat,' I added. 'More space.'

The woman turned and smiled, and the action of turning her head shook loose another tear. 'It's such a long time since I've seen my son,' she explained. 'He moved to Madrid eighteen years ago, and I'm so frightened of flying that I've never had the courage to go and see him. He always offered to pay, but – I'm such a silly old woman, me.' The coda came so naturally to her that I wondered if she used it often.

The woman sighed heavily. 'This time I couldn't put it off any longer. I think I was called, you know, by the Lord. I don't know if God's calling me to see my son, or if He's calling me home – but, if it's His will, there's no escaping it, is there?'

As if by design, her fingers, still fiddling with the crucifix, caught a beam of light, and directed it into my eyes. I felt a disproportionate annoyance: the last thing I wanted was to spend fourteen hours at the mercy of a tearful evangeliser. In an aeroplane there was no escape: one was a prisoner, a captive audience. People should realise how important it was not to impose their ideas on their neighbours.

'My only hope is that I don't die before I see my son and my grandchildren.' She delved under the constricting rug again to produce a tear-soaked handkerchief, and dabbed at her eyes. She repeated, and now I took the repetition to be meaningful: 'I haven't seen my son for eighteen years.'

Her son had left Argentina in 1977, so he must be a political exile. I felt a sort of relief, then, for this unknown escapee, and a new warmth towards his mother. So many other sons and daughters had stayed behind and died. Even now we were flying over the broad estuary of the River Plata, where hundreds, maybe thousands, of bodies lay and would probably lie for ever. The muddy river kept its secret as well as the forest.

As I thought about the bodies in the river, the empty seat beside me took on a significance, as if it represented a *desaparecido* who had not been able to leave. I smiled a secret understanding at my neighbour, whose son was safe, and she returned the smile, though not the solidarity that went with it. Her eyes registered no particular meaning.

'Do you live in Buenos Aires?' the woman asked.

'I've been living there, but I'm going home now.'

'What were you doing?'

'I was a foreign correspondent,' I said. 'I wasn't much good at it.'

The admission of failure drew a sympathetic smile from her. 'Is your family over there, in England?'

'Yes.'

'A family is a blessing, isn't it?'

She let go of the crucifix and delved into her handbag on the floor, finally retrieving a snapshot of a benign old man, taken in a summer garden full of flowers. 'This is my husband,' said the woman. 'He died a few years ago and I miss him so much. He would have loved to see our grandchildren in Madrid.'

The picture was out of focus, which seemed to confirm my first impression of the woman's bafflement. All the same, the blur of the flowers and the man's unfocused smile exuded a happiness that was heart-warming, so different from the stark, clinical photographs of the disappeared.

'He looks very nice,' I said. 'Very kind.'

'He was a gardener. He loved all his plants and things.'

That reminded me of Hugo. The day before leaving I had gone to say goodbye to him at the cemetery. We had found a tomb in the shade and exchanged books. I gave him a novel by Ernesto Sábato, an Argentine novelist I much admired, to whom Hugo had once introduced me, when we spotted the writer on the terrace of a café. 'The Argentine is unhappy with everything, and with himself,' wrote Sábato. 'There must be few countries in the world where such a feeling is so common.'

Hugo gave me a biography of W. H. Hudson. He told me about his ambition to start a plant nursery in Buenos Aires.

'But I would never want to give up my work here.' He looked affectionately at the surrounding tombs. All around us, the dead lay mulling over their lives.

'I'll miss Buenos Aires,' I said.

'You should live here,' said Hugo. 'You're melancholic like us.'

'That's precisely why I shouldn't live here.'

I unpacked the things I needed for the flight: a novel and if that proved too arduous, a magazine, and put these things on the empty seat. The woman, following my example, placed her handbag there. Between us, we quickly filled up the chair.

Now that she was released from her tartan cocoon, my neighbour was enjoying the many novelties of flight. Investigating the pouch, she had found the complimentary magazine and the sick bag, which caused her amusement at first, and then consternation, as she took in its full meaning. Clearly, she had worried so much about dying on the aeroplane, it had never crossed her mind to worry about being sick on it.

The free slippers she happily tucked into her capacious handbag and the meal, when it arrived, prompted even greater delight.

'What is this?' she asked, prodding the foil packet that represented a main course.

'According to the menu, it's Chicken Chasseur.'

Thrilled, she sampled the contents of each little box, before returning to eat the courses in their conventional order. It was the first time I had seen a passenger eat everything off her tray and I felt a certain superiority. 'She doesn't know the protocol,' I thought, 'she doesn't realise that you're meant to leave something.' The lemon towelette and the menu she stored in her handbag.

When her meal was finished, the woman stretched back in her seat, casually pushing the tray aside. Her tongue scouted around for any scraps of food that might be lodged between her teeth. She seemed relaxed now, about the flight.

I said, 'Did your husband do gardening for private clients, or did he work for the local authority?'

The woman's face was, for a moment, an uncomprehending blank. Then a smile of realisation dawned. 'Oh, I see what you mean, dear,' she said. 'No, no – gardening was just his hobby.'

'I'm sorry – I misunderstood,' I said, though there was no reason to apologise.

'The language, perhaps?' said the woman, smiling benevolently.

'No, not that, I simply thought—'

'My husband', she said, 'was a policeman.'

'A policeman? Oh.'

'Yes, he worked for the federal police, in Buenos Aires.'

'Oh, I see.'

We looked at one another across the empty seat, with embarrassment, both of us knowing that the disclosure of such information begged questions it would usually be impertinent to ask.

The woman said, quite deliberately: 'He was a *good* man.'

I nodded, and looked out of the window, as if this had been a casual exchange to which neither one of us need contribute more. In due course, I took up my magazine to read – but all the time I was thinking, what did 'good' mean, when the context was so terrible? That her husband had not killed, that he had done so, but only under orders? Was it possible to be good and to work alongside men who were evil? Or did she mean that he had killed, but that the killing itself was a good thing?

It angered me to think of this policeman who had gone home in the evening to enjoy his garden, having deprived other people of future pleasures. The familiar black-and-white faces floated back into my mind; I wondered if Carlos came across the pictures when reading the morning papers, and if he ever recognised his own victims among the faces. *Disappeared. Tortured. Where is she now?* Carlos might be in a position to answer that, and other questions.

The hours lapsed, and I did not speak to my neighbour again. Headphones were distributed for the films and she took a pair. I saw her fiddling ineptly with the control buttons in her arm-rest, and made a cool decision not to offer any help. Soon an American comedy was playing itself out mutely on the screen ahead of us, the exertions of hero and heroine easy enough to follow through their exaggerated expressions. The headsets around me emitted a modern buzz of competing languages. The man sitting in front of me was listening to buzzy jazz.

I read about sexual perversions in a women's magazine and, when that palled, I tried the novel for a bit – but I could not concentrate. Instead, I stared into the black sky and mulled over the life that awaited me in Britain. Once I was home, perhaps I would consider a career change. At a dinner-party a week before I left Buenos Aires someone had expressed incredulity that I was a journalist – 'You don't *look* like one!' she had cried – and ever since I had been plagued with a worry, not just about my looks but about the possibility that she was right and I was in the wrong job. I thought about the options opened to me by Eugenia de Chikoff's zodiac book: writer, nun, philosopher or travel agent. These held their attractions, indeed I had often considered the first two. Now it occurred to me that the last two were also possibilities; they might even be satisfactorily combined.

When the second American film ended, the woman in the aisle seat pulled her blanket up under her chin and made a face ready for repose. I watched her easy descent into sleep with irritation: she was supposed to be the nervous traveller, and I her consolation. Yet here she slept, her head lolling on the head-rest – and with all that might have been on her conscience – whereas I knew that I would be awake all the way to Europe.

When I was sure that she was not just dozing, I took my chance to study my neighbour. Sleep made her unattractive, her cheeks slackened and the drooping mouth amassed flesh under her chin. The way her hands were cupped in her lap, she looked ready to receive the body of Christ, ready for absolution. What if she were right, and God was calling her, us all, 'home'?

As an experiment, I dared to concentrate a contempt into the way I was looking at the woman. Did she not bear some responsibility, as a policeman's wife, for *la represión*? Here was a way to fix all the frustration and anger of the last two years on to someone who might deserve to be hated – and yet I found that I did not hate her.

Halfway across the ocean and through the night, half a world away from Buenos Aires, the real city started to retreat in my mind and became something like an emblem. I imagined it encompassed by a timeless dark. In this symbolic night, shanty-dwellers wandered through the city's empty avenues while dictators turned in their mahogany coffins. The disembodied faces at the morgue gasped in the dark at the injustice of their death.

I pictured Evita, whose womb was killing her, walking among sleeping children in the little republic she had made for them, and Borges walking blind among the books at the National Library, both of them yearning for things they could not have. Borges had lived in the air, Elsie said, and when the streets of a city held so much pain, perhaps it was best not to let your feet touch the ground. The writer who loved his city so much had finally chosen to be buried in Switzerland.

'Who really loves me?' Evita asked a friend, hours before she died. Among the notes she had written in her last days, someone found the scribbled question: 'Can an entire people be happy?'

Night soothed. A few hours of blank-out, then the day could start again, and perhaps this time it would be better, the queues would be shorter, the weather less oppressive. The night offered solace, and there were all-night tango stations for melancholics, there was therapy for the insomniacs. How many psychoanalysts would it take to make an entire people happy?

Argentina was an enigma, an infinite puzzle, like one of Borges' stories of labyrinths. Dozens of historians and philosophers had dwelled on its mystery and had not been able to find an explanation for how such a wealthy country, such an educated populace had come to so much harm. Did the fault lie with the scheming oligarchs, the immigrants, the economic dominance of Britain, the megalomania of the Peróns?

After the humiliation of the World Cup, one such commentator, Mariano Grondona, wrote that he sometimes wished Argentines were more like Anglo-Saxons. He pictured the British drinking whisky in the evening, quietly glowing at the thought of the day's ordered accomplishments. Latins, he wrote, had a morning culture. 'We thrive on the instant magic of a new beginning, the infinite horizon of promise. The afternoon brings weariness and disenchantment. Our dream has been over-ambitious. But so what? There'll be other mornings. There'll be another World Cup.'

Every morning in Argentina presented an opportunity to start afresh. If the cycle were repeated often enough, maybe it would start to work, the flaw would be routed. One day there would be an honest president, a good police force, incorruptible judges.

Buenos Aires was a city of sleepwalkers. It was a city, some said, that was finally waking up. What would the wakers make of all their dreams of wealth, their nightmares of oppression? What future would they forge?

I could not sleep, while Buenos Aires burned in my mind.

Hours later, though dawn had not broken, lights were flicked on to create an artificial morning. Bleary queues formed for the lavatories and the air hostesses appeared, freshly made up and smiling. Briskly they patrolled the aisles, like nurses among invalids, dispensing aspirins and orange juice. My neighbour awoke then from her deep sleep and looked about her with a blinking surprise. Meeting her eye, I smiled, though not yet generously.

We tackled our breakfast in silence, both absorbed by the tinned fruit and the ready-mix scrambled egg. The map charting our progress at the front of the cabin showed a cartoon aeroplane advancing edgily towards Morocco.

Soon dawn breathed a new blue into the sky. 'Oh, look at that,' said the woman, returning from the lavatory. 'I never imagined it could be so beautiful.'

'It's an experience no one should miss,' I agreed and, since we were talking, I asked her a question that had occurred to me during the night.

'What does your son do in Spain, out of interest?' It occurred to me now that he was not a political exile, as I had first thought. Why would he have needed to escape, if his father was a policeman?

'He's an engineer,' said the woman proudly. 'He was ever so lucky to get that job.'

In anticipation of our landing, the Spanish captain told us about the weather and temperature in Madrid. It was a crisp but sunny winter morning there, he said, admiring of his own country's climate. I was looking forward to the European winter after the intolerable heat of Buenos Aires. I hoped the cold winds would bring a clarity of mind. The captain suggested we might like to alter our watches to Spanish time, and my neighbour fumbled obediently with her strap.

Presently the aeroplane began to bob and drop.

'What's happening?' cried the woman.

'We're losing height,' I said, 'ready for the landing.'

'Oh my God!' One knobbly hand reached instinctively for the crucifix.

'There's nothing to it. You needn't worry.'

'No, no – I've read about this. It's the most dangerous bit, when all the accidents happen.'

As the mountains surrounding Madrid loomed into view, the woman became increasingly agitated. Every unfamiliar noise or movement she greeted with a whimper and the clunking drop of the landing gear made her jump in her seat. Uncertain how best to brace herself for the disaster she thought inevitable, the woman tried gripping the arm-rests, then the crucifix with both hands. She crossed herself obsessively. I was concerned to see her so frightened. The features I had observed slumped in sleep a few hours ago were alert now to a growing panic. She looked as if she could even become hysterical.

Finally I said: 'Look – take my hand.'

I extended my hand across the bags and books between us and, once again, the woman grasped it. Her fingers tightened on mine and I returned the pressure. Eyes tight shut, she began to mumble prayers and tears appeared at the corners of her eyes, but she was calmer now; the human contact was an anchor.

The aeroplane hung fast over the runway for some seconds, then landed smoothly, but it was not until the other passengers broke into cheerful applause that the woman realised she was out of danger. Then she opened her eyes and breathed deeply. She looked around her in amazement.

'Praise be to God,' she whispered, with the fervour of someone who had expected to die and now intended to savour the miracle of life.

'There you are,' I said, 'back on firm land.'

She smiled warmly at me. 'Thank you dear,' she said. She let go of my hand, then, impulsively, gave it a one last squeeze.

'We survived, didn't we? We survived!'

FURTHER READING

A note on translations. In quoting the Peróns, and several other public figures, I have used both my own translations and some made by previous authors, in particular Fraser and Navarro.

Borges, Jorge Luis, *Obras Completas* (Barcelona, 1989).

Borges, Jorge Luis, *Selected Poems 1923–1967* (London, 1972).

Chatwin, Bruce, *In Patagonia* (London, 1979).

CONADEP, *Nunca Más/Never Again* (A Report by Argentina's National Commission on Disappeared People. London, 1986).

Duarte, Erminda, *Mi Hermana Evita* (Buenos Aires, 1972).

Frank, Waldo, *América Hispana* (New York, 1931).

Fraser, Nicholas and Marysa Navarro, *Evita – The Real Lives of Eva Perón* (London, 1996).

Graham-Yooll, Andrew, *A State of Fear – Memories of Argentina's Nightmare* (London, 1986).

Hudson, W. H., *Far Away and Long Ago – A Childhood in Argentina* (London, 1918).

Martínez, Tomás Eloy, *Las Memorias del General* (Buenos Aires, 1996).

Martínez, Tomás Eloy, *Santa Evita* (London, 1997).

Naipaul, V. S., *The Return of Eva Perón* (London, 1980).

Nogués, Germinal, *Buenos Aires, Ciudad Secreta* (Buenos Aires, 1996).

Perón, Eva, *La Razón De Mi Vida* (Buenos Aires, 1951). English translation: *My Mission in Life* (New York, 1952).

Perón, Eva, *The Writings of Eva Perón* (New York, 1950).

Rock, David, *Argentina 1516–1987* (Berkeley and Los Angeles, 1987).

Salas, Horacio, *El Centenario – La Argentina En Su Hora Más Gloriosa* (Buenos Aires, 1996).

Sarmiento, Domingo, *Civilización y Barbarie: Vida de Juan Facundo Quiroga* (Mexico City, 1980).

Scalabrini Ortiz, Raúl, *El Hombre que está Solo y Espera* (Buenos Aires, 1931).

Shumway, Nicholas, *The Invention of Argentina* (Berkeley and Los Angeles, 1991).

Simpson, John and Jana Bennett, *The Disappeared* (London, 1986).

Timerman, Jacobo, *Prisoner without a Name, Cell without a Number* (London, 1981).

Walger, Sylvina, *Pizza con Champán – Crónica de la Fiesta Menemista* (Buenos Aires, 1994).

Walsh, Rodolfo, *A Year of Dictatorship in Argentina* (London, 1977).

Williamson, Edwin, *The Penguin History of Latin America* (London and New York, 1992).

Woodall, James, *The Man in the Mirror of the Book – A Life of Jorge Luis Borges* (London, 1996).